W9-AOA-165

"Ellen Dollar is a consummate storyteller with a consuming story to tell. She is also a gifted journalist. In *No Easy Choice*, she has combined those skills to produce a gripping account of her family's engagement with one of the pressing questions of our time: what and where is the Christian interface between humanity and the bioengineering we can—and now do—exercise on ourselves, our children-in-the-making, our species? Chock-full of informed and candid insights, this one is a page-turner."

—Phyllis Tickle, author of *The Divine Hours*

"This is a most thoroughgoing evaluation of questions that will absorb prospective parents, doctors, pastors, and those who counsel couples about in vitro fertilization and genetic testing. Anyone reading it will come away better informed on such vital choices challenging our culture."

—Virginia Stem Owens, author of *Caring for Mother*

"Prepare yourself for a compelling, moving, and difficult journey. Ellen Painter Dollar has reflected deeply on the ethics of reproduction for someone with a disabling genetic disorder. Part biography, part ethics, and part science, this book takes you through the hardest and deepest questions surrounding genetics and disability. It will make you weep and smile, think and react, and deepen your relationship with God. Elegantly written, this is a book of sheer genius born out of a story of pain, complexity, and faithfulness. This is book worth reading and rereading."

—The Very Rev. Dr. Ian Markham, Dean and President of
Virginia Theological Seminary, Professor of Theology and Ethics,
and author of more than twenty books, including *Do Morals Matter?*

"This book is a welcome antidote to dry academic reflection on the ethics of PGD. The author walks us through her difficult decisions about using reproductive technologies in the face of having her children inherit a painful medical condition, cutting through the certitudes of those who do not have to face these choices themselves. Those pondering the use of reproductive technologies and those concerned with the ethics of these technologies will benefit from reading this book."

—John H. Evans, Professor of Sociology, University of
California–San Diego, and author of *Contested Reproduction:
Genetic Technologies, Religion, and Public Debate*

"I have worked at the intersection of faith and disability for years, while keeping an eye open to the ethical, moral, spiritual, and theological issues arising from new developments in prenatal testing and assistive reproductive technologies. It seemed like an area with overwhelming complexity, hard to 'grab hold of.' Ellen Dollar has simply provided an amazingly clear path into that complexity, a path that other families, clergy, and health care professionals can use to understand the depth and nuances of the choices and decisions that involve faith, emotions, parenting, medicine, cultural values and personal/family identity. Her refusal to accept platitudes or easy either-or answers, combined with clear, nuanced explorations of each step in their journey, makes this a unique book and resource. It is much more than memoir and more like an extended "case story," but not one written by a health care professional or clergy in training. Rather, it turns the tables and is written by the 'case' herself, a parent of faith carrying a very risky gene who is trying to deal with the worlds of science, theology, and culture. I learned a lot and felt honored to be invited into the intimacy and capacity to deal with that wider intersection that happens at the beginning of life itself."

Bill Gaventa, MDiv
Associate Professor, Pediatrics,
The Elizabeth M. Boggs Center on Developmental Disabilities
UMDNJ-Robert Wood Johnson Medical School; former editor,
Journal of Religion, Disability, and Health

"In *No Easy Choice*, Ellen Painter Dollar sets out to provide a guide for Christians considering reproductive technology. She succeeds, and then some. Weaving together an honest and touching personal narrative with ethical and theological insight, Dollar writes about a complex topic in simple terms. *No Easy Choice* should provoke thought, prayer, and discussion from any Christian who wants to engage the most pressing ethical concerns of the twenty-first century."

—Amy Julia Becker, author of *A Good and Perfect Gift:
Faith, Expectations, and a Little Girl Named Penny*

"This book is both a challenge and a blessing for those who see the beauty that human disability brings to the world and the deep and troubling truths that it reveals about our societies. Moving, touching, personal, and filled with deep Christian spirituality, Dollar's book will move hearts and make a difference."

—John Swinton, Chair in Divinity and Religious Studies
and Professor in Practical Theology and Pastoral Care,
University of Aberdeen

No Easy Choice

No Easy Choice

A Story of Disability, Parenthood, and Faith in an Age of Advanced Reproduction

Ellen Painter Dollar

WESTMINSTER
JOHN KNOX PRESS
LOUISVILLE · KENTUCKY

First edition
Published by Westminster John Knox Press
Louisville, Kentucky

12 13 14 15 16 17 18 19 20 21—10 9 8 7 6 5 4 3 2 1

Book design by Sharon Adams
Cover design by designpointinc.com

Scripture quotations from the New Revised Standard Version of the Bible (NRSV) are copyright © 1989 by the Division of Christian Education of the National Council of the Churches of Christ in the U.S.A. and are used by permission.

Scripture quotations from *The Holy Bible, New International Version* (NIV) are copyright © 1973, 1978, 1984 International Bible Society. Used by permission of Zondervan Bible Publishers.

"The Way of Pain" © 1998 by Wendell Berry from *The Selected Poems of Wendell Berry*. Reprinted by permission of Counterpoint.

Library of Congress Cataloging-in-Publication Data
Dollar, Ellen Painter.
 No easy choice : a story of disability, parenthood, and faith in an age of advanced reproduction / Ellen Painter Dollar.
      p. cm.
 Includes bibliographical references (p.   ).
 ISBN 978-0-664-23690-8 (alk. paper)
 1. Human reproductive technology—Moral and ethical aspects. 2. Human reproductive technology—Religious aspects—Christianity. 3. Osteogenesis imperfecta. I. Title.
 RG133.5.D65 2012
 616.6'9206—dc23

                                                          2011039957

Most Westminster John Knox Press books are available at special quantity discounts when purchased in bulk by corporations, organizations, and special-interest groups. For more information, please e-mail SpecialSales@wjkbooks.com.

For Daniel, my best choice

For parents, the only way
is hard. We who give life
give pain. There is no help.
Yet we who give pain
give love; by pain we learn
the extremity of love.

—Wendell Berry, "The Way of Pain"

Contents

Acknowledgments

My theologian friend Chris Roberts, whose e-mailed counsel is included in *No Easy Choice*, first proposed that I write about my experience with PGD (preimplantation genetic diagnosis). He and his wife, Hannah, served as chief cheerleaders, connecting me with key people and reading the manuscript in various iterations. Chris introduced me to Phyllis Tickle, who championed my rough manuscript early on, and publicist Kelly Hughes, who suggested that I send my proposal to her friend Jana Riess, a new acquisitions editor at Westminster John Knox Press.

I was always envious (and a little skeptical) of authors who claimed that, after years of knocking at the doors of publishing powers-that-be, they finally connected with an agent or editor who was a perfect match. I was certain that such happy endings must be incredibly rare in a profession so rife with unfulfilled expectations. But now I am one of those writers gushing about how I found just the right partner for my publishing journey. Jana possesses a keen editorial eye, loads of common sense, and an approach to faith that manages to be at once smart and funny, earnest and irreverent, serious and amiable. She has been not just a fabulous editor, but also a mentor and kindred spirit. Jana worked with me for a year to refine my book proposal, patiently waiting as I learned to let go of things that I saw as necessary but she knew were not. I thank Jana and all the Westminster John Knox staff for taking a chance on an unknown author, an unusual format, and a controversial topic.

Before I found a home for this book, my moms' group/book group—six women whom I met when our oldest children were babies

xii   Acknowledgments

and who are the first people I call in any emergency—would perk up
my spirits by saying things like, "If [insert best-selling author's name
here] could get *this* nonsense published, we just don't understand
why you haven't found a publisher for your work, Ellen!" Tammy
Burns, Kate Byroade, Cathy Puleo, Jen Schaefer, Katey Scrimgeour,
and Carol Shilliday—for your kindness and everything else, from
welcoming my children into your homes as if they were your own
to our child-free strolls around Portsmouth and late-night glasses of
wine, thank you. They and many other friends and extended family
members, near and far, became loyal readers of my blog posts and
articles long before this book was finished. Thanks to all of you who
asked insightful questions, read and shared my online publications,
and were unfailingly generous with encouragement. Kristi Leon-
ard was an energetic and attentive caregiver for my son, Ben, many
afternoons, which gave me hours of uninterrupted time to write.

Ian Markham and Frank Kirkpatrick made helpful connections
and comments after reading an early draft. Stacy Sibley and Kat
Becker read the adoption section in chapter 2, and their suggestions
made it better. I "met" Amy Julia Becker online long before I met
her in person; as a writer covering similar territory, she has served as
colleague, editor, and friend.

A number of women answered my online call for people willing
to share the stories of their difficult reproductive decisions related to
prenatal diagnosis, pregnancy termination, genetic disorders, infertility, and adoption. Although not every story made it into this book,
they all made their way into my heart and mind. I won't thank them
by name because many requested anonymity, but I offer my deepest
thanks to these storytellers for informing my work with courage and
honesty.

Two of the best teachers I ever had, Professor David Holmes and
Professor James Axtell at the College of William and Mary, insisted
that student papers exhibit quality writing as well as sound arguments. They, along with the resources they shared (such as Strunk
and White's *Elements of Style* and William Zinsser's *On Writing
Well*), awakened in me a passion for precise word choice and well-
crafted sentences. Under their tutelage, I began to suspect I might be
a writer.

My parents, Ann and Borden Painter, helped with many nuts-and-bolts tasks related to this book, including watching my kids and being among my first (and most sympathetic) readers. But more important, they have always offered their support no matter how questionable the endeavor, from allowing me to take physical risks as a fragile child to encouraging me to continue writing this book without any assurance that anyone would ever read it.

Finally, to my husband, Daniel, and our children, Leah, Meg, and Ben: You accepted (graciously in Daniel's case, not always so graciously in the children's) my spending many hours holed up with the laptop or engaging in distracted conversations when my mind was clearly focused on my next paragraph instead of on you. I'm sure it has often felt that my writing this book has taken me away from you. I hope you will eventually understand that this book, and the story at its core, is one of the many things that bind us together. This is not just my story; it is our story. Thank you for allowing me to tell it.

Introduction

Making Choices When There Is No Easy Choice

Family Portrait: September 29, 2003

We have been in the emergency room for several hours and have reached that point when things are calm, almost—unbelievably—relaxing. My nearly four-year-old daughter, Leah, is lying on a gurney next to me, spaced out on sedatives and pain relievers and watching a *Winnie the Pooh* video for the third time. I am digging peanut M&M's out of my purse, eating them slowly, one by one, so the nurses and doctors going in and out won't think me insensitive for chowing down on vending-machine food while my daughter lies there pale and defeated. Now that we are beyond the worst—the first harrowing moments of knowing that Leah has just broken another bone (this time both left forearm bones, so unmistakably, heartsinkingly broken, bent at a 45-degree angle), the anxious conversations with the triage nurses, the IV and X-ray and sedation and casting—I need a sugar rush.

The staff at the children's hospital have all commented on my pregnant belly, asking me if I know what we're having (another girl) and if I'll be delivering the baby across the street at the main city hospital. Yes, I answer—though the hushed, dark-paneled delivery suites seem, at this moment, miles away from this bright room where crutches of all sizes hang from wall pegs as flat-headed, one-legged observers of children in anguish and parents aching over their little ones' broken limbs. But those delivery suites are not so far away after all. Our baby will be born there in just four days.

The pivotal times in our journey toward having a second baby were always, it seemed, accompanied by one of Leah's fractures. So this ER visit just a few days before I was to give birth fit the pattern. I tried to read meaning into this coincidence, which was probably a silly exercise given how often Leah broke bones during the two years when we were so focused on having a second baby. But maybe it wasn't so silly, because our decisions about our second child revolved around Leah and her diagnosis of osteogenesis imperfecta (OI), a genetic disorder better known as "brittle-bone disease." Frequent broken bones, often as the result of little or no trauma, are the hallmark of OI.

Leah did not walk until she was two-and-a-half because of weakness in her muscles and joints. Because she was not fully mobile, she was spared bone fractures for her first two years. In fact, her first fracture happened on her second birthday, when she fell while climbing on her new child-size couch—purchased explicitly to provide a safer alternative to climbing around on the full-size couch. I could not make up a more appropriate introduction to the illogical, unpredictable nature of this disorder. Kids with OI can have spectacular falls and be fine, and they can break bones during the most mundane activities, like climbing around on a minicouch.

When Leah finally started walking several months after that fracture healed, she also started falling and broke three bones in three months that first summer she was mobile. We then had a glorious nine months without a fracture, during which she started preschool and became truly active for the first time in her life. Then summer came again—a fracture of the tibia and fibula (both lower leg bones) in June, followed by the broken arm that landed us in the ER four days before our second daughter's birth. Both of these last fractures were gruesome, ugly things, with bones bent at stomach-turning angles and huge bruises instantly swelling and discoloring her tender skin. Like most of her other fractures, they both happened in our living room when I was within arm's reach.

Like other parents, I worry about my children out in the world: Will they remember to look both ways when they cross the street? Do they understand that when I say, "Never go anywhere with anyone without asking Mom or Dad if it's OK," I really mean *never*, even if the guy down the street asks you to help him find his lost puppy? But unlike other parents, I cannot assume a relative absence of risk even when my daughter is playing in the living room while I leaf through the L. L. Bean catalog nearby. Neither my proximity nor the familiar confines of home can protect Leah from breaking.

Between her second and fourth birthdays, Leah had six broken bones. As much as I hated the harrowing hours following each fracture, they were a crisis, so I was propelled by adrenaline. The days and weeks that followed offered no such boost. I became weary and sad. The routines we hardly thought about in healthy times became dreaded chores, requiring brute strength and mental gymnastics. How to carry her—leg sticking straight out and encased in purple fiberglass—into our narrow bathroom, get her pants down, and sit her on the toilet with her leg elevated, all without hurting her?

We had to adjust to how this fracture would change our plans. The disappointments piled up, each one surprising me more than it should have. I kept forgetting that we inhabited a different world now, one in which making plans was foolhardy and the simplest of childhood rituals, from playing in the bathtub to attending a birthday party without Mom, were forbidden. There would be no swimming for Leah during our vacation to sweltering eastern North Carolina, where relatives run a church camp and have a swimming hole fifty yards from their front door. Our brand-new swing set, with its sturdy wide steps and not-too-high slide, chosen especially for Leah's safety, sat empty and unused for most of the first summer we owned it. Each loss carved a chunk out of the optimism and faith I tried to cultivate in sunnier times. My pain was that of observer and absorber of my child's agony. Leah did not talk about being sad, but she flew into rages more easily than usual, reverted to an arm-flapping ritual that she developed as a baby and wailed when I demanded that we make a trip to the bathroom because she hadn't gone in five hours.

In this postfracture state, I inevitably questioned my desire for another child. The sheer logistics seemed overwhelming. Caring for a child with a newly broken bone while caring for other children is a challenge many parents have met—once or twice, maybe. But we could potentially be in this position several times a year for the next 10, 12, or 14 years. And we could easily have another child with OI. Because I have OI too, there is a 50 percent chance that any child of mine will inherit it. Any sane person, you would think, would have left well enough alone. I had a smart, beautiful daughter, healthy in all ways save her fragile bones. The thing is, I am sane—practical, level-headed, deliberate, thoughtful. I should have just accepted that one child was enough. But I could not. My husband, Daniel, could not.

As Leah was going through her relentless fracture cycle, Daniel and I were picking our way along a tangled and twisted path toward having another baby. We confronted questions—many of them unanswerable—concerning medicine, family, faith, and the reproductive choices available to twenty-first-century Americans with even a modest amount of disposable income. We struggled and cursed. We prayed and talked and e-mailed. And so we ended up in the ER that night, a child's broken arm and a woman's pregnant belly linked in ways no casual observer could imagine, leading characters in the mundane and extraordinary life that our family has been given.

A Hard and Lonely Time

Much of this book is the story of the months that preceded that night in the ER and our second daughter's birth later that week, although telling that story requires telling other stories as well. There is the story of my own fragile childhood and the scars it left on body, mind, and spirit, understanding that scars are both permanent reminders of life-altering pain and proof that what is broken can be restored, even if it will never be the same as it once was. There is the story of how having babies has shaped my body, my faith, my writing, and all the painful and redemptive places where those things have become entwined with each other.

But while these stories form the heart of this book, *No Easy Choice* is not only a memoir. When Daniel and I set out on that twisted, tangled path toward having a second baby, we did so largely on our own. We had doctors and genetic counselors who skillfully explained how the relatively new technology known as preimplantation genetic diagnosis (PGD)—in vitro fertilization (IVF) with the added step of testing fertilized eggs for specific genetic mutations—could allow us to conceive our future children in a laboratory and thus guarantee that they would not inherit the genetic mutation that caused my and Leah's OI. We had family members, friends, and pastors willing to listen as we talked about the difficult questions that PGD raised for us. Some of the questions were relatively straightforward: How would we pay for the procedure? Was I willing to bear the physical discomfort and emotional stress of IVF and PGD, with all the hormone injections, surgery, and medical monitoring? The ongoing support of our families, particularly our parents, helped us to answer those sorts of questions.

Many of our questions, however, were much more fraught and complex: By using PGD to ensure OI-free children, were we diminishing the inherent value of people like me, Leah, and others living with disabilities? Why were we so intent on avoiding OI in additional children when Leah and I offer proof that life with this disorder can be rich and happy? And what about our Christian faith? By discarding embryos with the OI mutation, would we be committing murder? Was it ethical to spend thousands of dollars to conceive a healthy child when millions of children don't have enough to eat or basic health care? What does our faith have to say about the suffering of illness and disability, and how far we should go to avoid it? Doesn't Christ's suffering on the cross show us that suffering can bring about life-giving transformation? We knew we wanted more children, but did that desire stem from God's call or from our selfish wants? How do the values that govern reproductive and genetic medicine compare with Christian values? In short, how could we, as Christians, make sound moral decisions about whether or not to use IVF and PGD?

We discussed our dilemma with a few other Christians. With one notable exception (which I will discuss later in the book), those we consulted, while kind and wise, were as perplexed as we were. None of us even knew exactly which ethical questions were most important, much less where and how to seek answers. It was a hard and lonely time.

Given the intimacy and weight of childbearing decisions, it would likely have been a somewhat hard and lonely time even if we had the most compassionate, informed counselors and resources possible at our side. Yet I'm also convinced that we—Christians called to bear one another's burdens and offer wisdom and support to our brothers and sisters—can make complex, difficult childbearing decisions less lonely and less hard for fellow believers considering whether or not to use reproductive technologies such as IVF and PGD. Doing so requires us to understand the current and potential uses of reproductive technology and the many moral questions it raises, and then consider how Christian faith might inform answers to those questions. This book is a tool for those interested, for personal or professional reasons, in furthering such understanding.

My family's story forms the core of this book. But I've gone beyond our story to more broadly consider and discuss the ethical questions our situation raised—questions that are increasingly relevant and vital as reproductive technologies become more sophisticated, available, and commonplace. I am not a theologian, bioethicist, or pastor. I am someone with a story about making tough choices concerning whether or not to use reproductive technology. I have written the sort of book I wish Daniel and I had when we were mired in terribly difficult decisions, with few resources to help us climb out of the muck; we were consumed with caring for a fragile toddler while deciding whether and how to have a second baby, given the 50 percent chance that baby would also be fragile. This book is a resource not only for other parents or parents-to-be who are deciding whether and how to have babies but also for those called to support and counsel them, including family and friends, pastors and counselors. I also hope that professionals who have a voice in cultural debates about the potential, limits, and pitfalls of reproductive technology—doctors, nurses, genetic counselors, bioethicists, theologians—will find in this book some valuable insights into how medical, ethical, and theological principles intersect with the day-to-day realities of family life.

"We Have to Consider the Quality of Our Children"

In 2010, British biologist Robert G. Edwards won the Nobel Prize in medicine for his contribution to the development of in vitro fertilization (IVF) technology more than thirty years earlier. Edwards and his late research partner, Patrick Steptoe, pioneered the process by which the first so-called test-tube baby was born in 1978. Since then an estimated four million babies worldwide have been born as a result of IVF, in which embryos are created from eggs and sperm in a laboratory and then implanted in a woman's uterus. As of this writing, here in the United States that process leads to the live birth of one or more infants about 30 percent of the time.

Media coverage of Edwards's prize was noticeably superficial. Major media outlets known for rigorous reporting cited all those healthy babies and happy parents as proof that ethical concerns about reproductive technology are passé. NPR's Robert Siegel began an interview with bioethicist Jeffrey Kahn by asking, "Have four million births through IVF trumped all the moral and ethical questions that were posed by the procedure?" Other news stories failed to address ethical questions at all, portraying Edwards as a brave pioneer who fought back against uptight alarmists. A *New York Times* article, for example, stated:

> Advances in human reproductive technology arouse people's deepest concerns and often go through a cycle, first of outrage and charges of playing God, then of acceptance. In vitro fertilization proved no exception. "We know that I.V.F. was a great leap because Edwards and Steptoe were immediately attacked by an unlikely trinity—the press, the pope, and prominent Nobel laureates," said the biochemist Joseph Goldstein in presenting the Lasker Award to Dr. Edwards in 2001. . . . The objections [to IVF] gradually died away—except on the part of the Roman Catholic Church—as it became clear that the babies born by in vitro fertilization were healthy and that their parents were overjoyed to be able to start a family.

When Edwards received his Nobel Prize, I was finishing this book, which is the culmination of a seven-year process of using my family's story as a springboard for examining the many ethical questions posed by modern reproductive technology. I knew there was much more to the Edwards story than most media outlets reported.

I knew, for example, that the existence of all those happy families does not trump moral inquiry. Parental joy with their healthy IVF-conceived babies, while compelling and understandable, does not negate ethical concerns. I also knew that Roman Catholic leaders, while providing the most consistent and thorough Christian position on reproductive technology, are far from the only ones concerned with the moral questions it raises. Theologians from various religions, as well as bioethicists, journalists, bloggers, and regular folk faced with complex reproductive decisions regularly engage in lively, rigorous discussions about the moral implications of established and emerging technologies. Rather than the ethical questions raised by IVF diminishing as the technique has become commonplace, the number of ethical questions has actually grown as reproductive technologies—not only IVF, but also PGD, prenatal diagnosis, sperm and egg donation, and surrogacy—have become more sophisticated and ubiquitous.

I also knew the deep-seated contentment of being a mother. I knew how it felt to hold a baby in the glow of warming lights minutes after she emerged from my body. I knew the grateful amazement of realizing that the doctors and nurses were going to *let me bring this baby home, to keep!* I knew the visceral, fundamentally human desire for a child of one's own, the heartache when that desire goes unfulfilled, and the joy when it is met.

But even knowing what I knew, as I continued to write about ethical concerns in the midst of the media's uncritical assessment of Edwards's accomplishments and the compelling portraits of happy families, I felt a little like the overly chatty aunt at a family wedding—the one who keeps reminding everyone that 50 percent of marriages end in divorce and pointing out all the ways that the new husband and wife are polar opposites.

But I kept on writing because I also knew something else about Robert Edwards, something that appeared in very few of the news stories about his Nobel Prize. In 1999, Edwards did an interview with London's *Sunday Times*, in which he said, "Soon it will be a sin of parents to have a child that carries the heavy burden of genetic disease. We are entering a world where we have to consider the quality of our children."

Edwards was referring to the use of PGD, which allows embryos created through IVF to be tested for genetic mutations, most commonly for those causing genetic disorders that affect children, such as Tay-Sachs disease, cystic fibrosis, Down syndrome, or my own genetic disorder, OI. In addition, PGD can be used to detect mutations for adult-onset diseases with a genetic component (such as Alzheimer's, Huntington's, and breast cancer) and genes for nondisease traits such as eye color, as well as to determine whether an embryo is male or female. Clinicians and parents can thus select embryos with or without a particular trait to be implanted into a woman's uterus.

On the surface, PGD is a straightforward medical technique. It gives families with a history of genetic anomalies, like mine, an opportunity to banish the physical and emotional pain of a disorder from their family forever. But Edwards's statement about PGD reveals the potential for this technology to be used and misused in ways that could forever alter our perspective on sickness and health, parental choice and responsibility, and traits that make a human being valuable. Edwards's use of the word "sin" raises the terrible possibility that parents will bear ultimate responsibility for their children's health—and be punished (by having essential medical or educational services withheld from their disabled children, for example) if they choose *not* to use available technology to ensure genetically healthy offspring. His use of the word "quality" makes clear how reproductive technology tempts us to commodify our children and transform them from gifts to be welcomed as they are, to products manufactured to parental and cultural specifications, literally subjected to quality control.

Will reproductive technologies such as PGD inevitably lead us down a slippery slope to a *Brave New World* society in which children are produced to meet the criteria set by a consumer society? Not necessarily. In this book I argue that these technologies pose significant moral questions that deserve our attention. I also encourage readers to pay attention to the stories of parents who have used IVF, PGD, and other reproductive technologies. Although egregious abuses of and dangerous attitudes toward such technologies exist, the stories of those who use these technologies are often the stories of loving, thoughtful parents who made the best decisions they could, given their circumstances—parents who love their children as gifts to be accepted as they are, not as engineered products.

Why Christians Need to Be Part of the Conversation

Christians have a particular duty to explore the ethical questions around reproductive technology. Jesus preached about the need to embrace the most vulnerable people, "the least of these," including children and those excluded from society because of physical or mental illness, as well as poverty, gender, or occupation. At the heart of a Christian worldview is our valuing other human beings based not on their "quality"—their health, intelligence, appearance, or accomplishments—but rather based on their creation in the image of a loving God. I am quite certain that, if he were to become incarnate in twenty-first-century America, Jesus would focus on a multitude of modern sins, but bearing a child with a genetic disorder would not be among them.

When a Nobel prizewinner uses terms like "sin" and the "quality" of human beings in relation to the technology he has developed, it is clear that the technology is not value-neutral. Christians have an important role to play in the ongoing conversations, public and private, about reproductive ethics and technology, for reasons both theological and practical. We adhere to a radical theology that posits the worth of every human being. We follow a God who, by suffering and dying on the cross, showed us that suffering is part of the human condition, avoidance of suffering is not our highest moral imperative, and suffering can even bring about transformation. And yet Jesus' example also calls us to have compassion for those who suffer. It is impossible to take seriously the stories of those facing long-term infertility or disabling genetic conditions without feeling compassion and empathy for the burdens they bear, as well as hope and joy when medical technology helps them to have a longed-for healthy child.

From a practical standpoint, as reproductive technology becomes more capable and commonplace, more and more Christians sitting in the church pews on a Sunday morning will face decisions about whether and how to use those technologies, and not always for medical reasons. Increasingly fertility clinics are offering (and patients are requesting) technological reproduction techniques not because they have been diagnosed with infertility or have a genetic disorder, but because they want to ensure that they have a boy or a girl, they want to postpone childbearing until they are financially stable, or they are in a same-sex partnership. Prenatal screening for a host of genetic and other disorders (involving blood tests, high-level ultrasounds, amniocentesis, and other genetic tests) has become not just commonplace but expected of parents-to-be, so that more couples face difficult decisions about what to do when they learn that their unborn child has a potential or actual abnormality.

Today Christians considering whether and how to use reproductive technology for any of these reasons are largely alone with their decisions and have few accessible resources for ethical reflection. The media and popular culture have normalized reproductive technology. Now that we all know someone who has had a beautiful baby via IVF, it must be no big deal, right? Pastors, often unfamiliar with the technologies or the many-layered moral questions they raise, may fall back on inadequate, worn arguments pulled from the pro-choice or pro-life movements, depending on their political and theological persuasion. Medical personnel—the genetic counselors and fertility doctors whom people meet during their exploration of reproductive technology—at best often fail to adequately address the ethical concerns raised by the technology they offer, providing few resources and little encouragement for ethical deliberation. At worst, they provide incomplete or skewed information based on their personal bias (toward terminating or not terminating a pregnancy after a difficult prenatal diagnosis, for example, or toward higher-tech versus lower-tech assisted reproduction techniques), making already-fraught decisions that much harder for patients.

About This Book

All those involved in reproductive decision making—primarily aspiring parents but also their friends, family, pastors, counselors, and medical providers—are this book's intended audience. I believe the most effective ethical inquiry focuses on the front end of the decision-making process, not the back end. In other words, while I will use my own story and the stories of other parents to illustrate quandaries and raise questions, I'm not interested in judging decisions that have already been made, but in informing decisions that are yet to be made. I hope to equip those who are facing or may face complex reproductive decisions, and those who counsel and support them, to give deliberate and informed consideration to the moral aspects of their decisions. And I hope to fill a gaping hole in the resources and literature available to those making reproductive decisions.

Much of the literature on reproductive ethics is written by theologians or bioethicists. They know their stuff and have valuable insights to offer, but those insights are often shrouded in dry, academic prose. I am the educated daughter of a college professor, but for writing to engage both my head and my heart (and when we're talking about having babies, both head and heart must be engaged), I need it to tell a story in captivating, accessible language. Much academic or religious literature in this field lacks both story and accessibility.

News media tend to cover reproductive technology in one of two ways. As with the coverage of Edwards's Nobel, they present reproductive technology as a done deal, a fact of life, beyond the need for question or concern. Alternatively, news articles highlight the sensational and extraordinary—the tabloid-worthy Nadya Suleman "Octomom" story and unusual cases where women serving as surrogates fight to keep the babies they give birth to, or young fertile couples decide to create and freeze embryos to be implanted down the road when the timing appears optimal. Such stories have a place. They illustrate that there may indeed be a "slippery slope"; that widespread acceptance of technological reproduction to address infertility and genetic disorders can lead people to use it in other, potentially troubling ways; and that conceiving babies in laboratories does not banish the raw, unpredictable power of human emotion from the procreative process. But these sensational stories do little to advance useful public conversation about reproductive ethics. People tend to be either outraged or fall back on "Who am I to judge?" and then move on. By telling their stories, a few memoirists have reminded readers that reproductive decisions aren't black-and-white judgments and deserve more than knee-jerk reactions. But because memoirs are focused on an individual or family's unique circumstances, they have limited utility for people seeking counsel and information for their own reproductive decisions.

In *No Easy Choice* I have included what is most useful and compelling from each of these genres—discussion of key moral and theological principles, journalism, and memoir. Each chapter begins with a glimpse of my own journey as someone with a genetic disorder who chose to have biological children and wrestled with whether or not to use technology to do so. Chapter 6 is purely a memoir, but the other chapters go beyond memoir to engage a key set of ethical and theological questions raised by my story. For example, the memoir portion of chapter 1 focuses on my experience of growing up with a disabling and painful genetic disorder, and parenting a child with the same disorder. The rest of the chapter discusses theological and ethical questions related to disability and suffering, such as whether God intends or allows suffering and how our culture values or devalues people with disabilities.

Other chapters focus on the role of choice, desire, and vocation in people's decisions to become parents; cultural pressures on parents to raise children with certain qualities that will optimize their health and success; the effects of how the market orientation of fertility medicine influences the clinical culture in which practitioners and patients make treatment decisions; and our viewpoints on human embryos. In these substantive chapters, I incorporate numerous academic, theological, and journalistic resources, using accessible language to discuss their applicability for regular people making real-life decisions. Finally, I end each chapter with a list of questions for readers to further reflect on how what they have read might inform their own choices or perspective.

My goal in writing this book is to raise good questions and provide resources to help readers consider and answer those questions. Though I offer my opinion on particular situations, arguments, or technologies, I do not conclude by stating a clear position for or against Christians' use of reproductive technologies. As the title makes clear, I don't believe there was a clear "easy choice" for me and my family, nor is there a clear best choice for others facing complex childbearing decisions. I simply hope that this book and the resources provided in the bibliography offer information, insight, and support to make these tough choices just a little easier.

1

Fear of Falling

Seeking God in Suffering and Disability

When I was eight years old, my best friend Carrie's mom gave birth to her little sister, and I wrote in my diary, "I want to have a baby someday." Even then I knew that my words were stunted and fuzzy representations of something massive and solid. Being a mother was not just something I wanted to do; it was who I was supposed to be.

But my genes and my bones argued otherwise. OI is an autosomal dominant genetic disorder. An autosomal disorder involves a genetic mutation that is not sex-linked; it affects boys and girls equally. All genes come in pairs, with one in each pair inherited from each parent. With a dominant genetic disorder such as OI, only *one* gene of the pair has to be defective for a child to have the disorder. The defective gene, in other words, "dominates" the normal gene. I have one normal gene for producing type 1 collagen, a protein that gives bones resiliency and strength, and one defective gene. Any child I conceive inherits one or the other of these genes, plus a healthy type 1 collagen gene from my husband. A child who inherits my defective gene has OI. A child who inherits my healthy gene does not have OI. So there is a 50 percent chance that any child of mine, boy or girl, will inherit OI.

Being caused by a dominant mutation, OI is often passed from parent to child. But neither my mother nor my father have OI. My OI was caused by a new, or spontaneous, mutation; I am the first person in my family to have it. The OI mutation means that my body produces only half the normal amount of type 1 collagen, leading to fragile bones, loose joints, scoliosis, muscle weakness, and slightly smaller than average stature. There are more severe

15

forms of OI; children with these forms are often born with broken bones and have significant short stature, major bone deformities (C-shaped arm and leg bones, severe scoliosis), and dozens or hundreds of fractures. One very severe form is fatal within hours or days of birth.

Understanding my genes' potential to wreak havoc on my children's skeletons, I approached my desire for motherhood with a host of dark fears. I could not imagine reliving my own painful history with OI through my child—or perhaps I could, which was worse. It's not that I was an unhappy child; my life was flooded with good fortune. When I was six months old, not yet diagnosed with the disorder that would force its way into our family, we moved to a modest white clapboard house in a friendly neighborhood, with the elementary school almost literally in our backyard. Our town boasted of quality schools, a quaint town center, and attractive colonials on quarter-acre lots. When I was young, my mother (a registered nurse) stayed home to care for us while my father worked his way up the academic ladder as a history professor at Trinity College in Hartford, Connecticut. Money was tight (my mother reminds me that she used to borrow back our allowances at the end of the month for groceries), but we had a comfortable home, food and clothes, pets, a week on Cape Cod every summer, and the reassuring presence of loving and sensible parents. Dinner was at six, the bills were paid, the cars serviced, the beds made, the garden fertile.

In February 1969, just weeks after our move to that white clapboard house, my older sister, Beth, not quite two years old, wandered into the road. My mother, with me on her hip, ran to scoop her up. I started crying and did not stop. A trip to the emergency room revealed a spiral fracture of my left femur, the result of my leg being bent into an awkward position during my mom's street rescue. The orthopedist who treated me noticed that the sclerae, the whites of my eyes, were bluish—a common sign associated with OI, though it can also occur in healthy infants. That, combined with the fracture occurring with such little trauma and my bones appearing somewhat translucent on X-rays, led to his diagnosing me with OI.

We were very lucky that an orthopedist who knew something about OI was the one to examine me during that first visit to the emergency room. With children who have severe OI, it is obvious from birth (or now, with regular ultrasounds during pregnancy, before birth) that something is not right. But children with mild or moderate OI often look healthy. Parents like mine, who have no idea that their child has OI, bring their healthy-looking toddler to the ER, explaining that the child broke an arm or leg after a routine fall or saying that the baby has been crying a lot and they don't know why. The discovery of a broken femur or collarbone, along with old, untreated fractures showing up on X-ray, can lead to suspicion of child abuse. My doctor's quick diagnosis spared my parents and me that particular ordeal.

I do not remember the details of every one of my fractures— about three dozen altogether—but a few of particular menace leap out from the fog of memory. I sat down on the tiled bathroom floor, tucking my legs under me, to talk with my visiting grandmother as she brushed her hair in front of the mirror—and my femur snapped. I stepped down the small step from our dining room into our den, and my tibia buckled under me. My sister and I were playing tag in the backyard, me using crutches and wearing full-length metal leg braces. My foot slipped on the wet grass, and I went sprawling, both femurs giving way. I tripped on the phone cord and landed on my elbow, which shattered. The shattered elbow was the last one—not the last fall, but the last fall that led to a fracture. I was 11 years old, about to be saved by puberty. While OI is an incurable, lifelong condition, fractures often lessen after puberty, when bones are not quite so stressed by the rapid growth of early childhood.

In the years since then, my body has grown stronger. I still have long, shiny scars on my legs from repeated childhood surgery to insert metal rods that helped stabilize my femurs and tibias. Though I am a giant by OI standards, I stand barely four feet and eight inches tall. My barrel-shaped torso and left leg are shortened, and my right leg and my arms are the only parts of me the size they should be— together giving me an oddly squished and crooked look. My spine is curved and my joints ache, but I go about my business. I take walks. I lug grocery bags. I wear regular shoes, fitted with a small lift on the left shoe to partially correct my leg-length discrepancy. Buying shoes, *any shoes I want*, is still a thrill after so many years when hard-soled leather oxfords were my only choice because they were the only kind that would hook onto my leg braces. My choices are still limited to flat, supportive shoes—no high-heeled, pointy-toed boots will ever peek out from under my jeans—but having any choice at all still makes me feel a little giddy.

Psalm 51:8 says, "The bones you have broken will rejoice" (cf. KJV). These bones of mine have learned to dance, swirling in a hot dormitory attic or swaying self-consciously against my new husband on our wedding day. They have learned to climb evergreen-scented hiking paths, to carry children anchored on a hip, to dig up clots of soil to make a new garden bed. But rejoice? That they find a bit harder. They are still afraid of falling.

So much of what is hard about OI involves a loss of control. That is what the falls were, a loss of control over body that led to further loss of control as I became an invalid. My final surgeries, to replace the metal rods in my legs one last time, took place just before I entered the seventh grade. Though still and always small for my age, I had become too big for my parents to carry up and down the stairs in the hip spica casts (casts that covered the entire lower body, from chest to toes) that were standard postoperative procedure then. I whiled away my recovery on a rented hospital bed in our den, watching reruns of *Maude* and *The Jeffersons,* calling in to radio stations to win prizes, reading *Seventeen* magazine. I spent hours looking at the models in those magazines, leaning their softly waved blonde heads against a boyfriend's Shetland-wool sweater, convinced I could be just like them—from the clear skin and shiny hair to the boy to lean on—as soon as I got rid of all this plaster. Until then, I had to call for help when I wanted to change the channel, when I wanted to wash my hair, when I wanted a snack, when I had to go to the bathroom. In the years that followed, the fractures receded. No more plaster, no more hospital beds. I could pee when I wanted.

I began to cherish the control I had, the freedom from having to ask for help. And I became terrified of losing that freedom again. The fear of falling remained, quite literally, in my bones.

From my first day of seventh grade—even though I arrived weeks after the school year had started, still recovering from surgery, in a wheelchair and with a cast—I was okay. I knew I looked different from everyone else and wished I didn't, but I was okay. Once I recovered from that final operation, I stopped breaking. Wheelchairs, spica casts, and hospitalizations faded into unpleasant memories.

One day in eighth grade, I went to school, put my crutches into my locker, and never used them again.

But though my body no longer broke, it screamed out my fragile history every time I walked across a room, swaying side to side on mismatched legs, one nearly two inches shorter than the other. Every summer I donned shorts and bathing suits, feeling vulnerable as an earthworm crawling across a driveway in the hot sun, with my scars and wobbly, toneless flesh for all to see. When I posed for a picture with my friends, I tried to use my long arms—one part of my body that appeared unaffected by OI—to hide my crookedness, the right hip that jutted out too far, the spine that crumpled down onto my hips.

I navigated being a teenager by adopting a contradictory mix of shame and defiance. I was convinced that everyone noticed my scars, skinny legs, and lumpy back before noticing anything else, every single time they saw me. But I always accepted invitations to coed beach trips where my imperfections would be on full display. I tried out for every drama production in high school, knowing I would get some bit part as an old lady or a bystander, and yet did well enough when trying out for the lead role in the musical *Oliver!* that the director included me in the final callbacks. I did not get the part, and circumspect comments from a favorite teacher hinted that my inability to convincingly play a robust, able-bodied young boy affected that decision. Though I suspected, and experience seemed to confirm, that most young men would have a hard time seeing a tiny, crooked, and limping girl as anything but a trusty sidekick, in ninth grade I insisted that my first crush, a good friend, meet me after school one day for a grueling conversation to confirm that he didn't want to date me. As a high school senior, I approached another friend at his locker one morning to invite him to our prom, determined that I wouldn't sit at home on the big night.

On the rare occasion when someone made an issue of my disability—as with the failed attempt to play Oliver or when a classmate referred to me as a "cripple"—both male and female friends defended me graciously. But when I think of those years, I picture myself on the periphery, always the observer. One year I went bowling with girlfriends on Valentine's Day because none of us was dating anyone. I felt incredibly lucky that night because I could pretend, for a few hours, that my friends and I were the same. We were just a bunch of girls temporarily without boyfriends. I could forget that being without a boyfriend was not temporary for me, but always. That's how it was in high school, in college, and when I moved to Washington, D.C., after graduation.

In college, one of my closest friends started dating a young woman who was part of the Christian fellowship group that was our social center. She was no great beauty, but oh, how I envied her feet. When we all dressed in shimmery dresses and shoes for a spring dance, I looked longingly at her slim feet in their royal blue pumps, the slight prominence of her ankle above the soft leather, the little rounded bump at the top, over her instep. Such lovely structure in those feet. Even in black dress shoes, my feet were clumsy, flat, collapsed. The plastic braces I wore distorted my shoes; they were no longer the sleek and refined things their designer had meant them to be. I was convinced that my life would be different with prettier feet. Would my friend have loved me instead of her if my feet were different? I felt sure that he would have.

My life has been abundantly full. I have a painful disorder, but I have also had access to excellent medical care. I had many lonely and sometimes hopeless years when I was certain no one would ever choose me as a partner, but I always had a supportive family and fabulous friends. And I did eventually get married to the person I would rather be with than anyone else in the world.

Yet all that good fortune, while certainly making life better than bearable, does not cancel out the significant pain, physical and otherwise, that OI brought me. How am I to view that pain in light of my Christian faith? Does it have any meaning that I need to pay attention to? Is OI a reflection of God's will for me, my particular cross to bear? Or does God desire my healing as much as I do? Questions like these come to all believers at one point or another; all human beings know pain. Given the very tangible suffering that many people with genetic disorders live with, including both physical pain and social stigma, these questions take on special urgency for Christians considering whether it is ethical to use reproductive and genetic technology to avoid having children with genetic anomalies.

Genetic Disorders and the Nature of Suffering

Writer and theologian Amy Julia Becker, reflecting on whether her daughter with Down syndrome will still have an extra chromosome 21 in heaven, believes she might, "because any aspect of that extra chromosome causing separation—physical, emotional, relational— will be overcome." In Becker's experience, her daughter Penny's Down syndrome has caused little intrinsic suffering or disability. Yet Penny lives in a culture that insists on seeing her as sick and flawed, even though her daily life is hardly different from that of any other preschooler. Becker insists that "much of the alienation and stigma people with disabilities experience is a product of societal norms rather than of problems intrinsic to the disabilities themselves." She concedes, however, that while her daughter has suffered little, children and adults with some conditions do indeed suffer a great deal.

Likewise, theologian Stanley Hauerwas acknowledges how our perception that people with disabilities suffer greatly is skewed by cultural assumptions valuing independence and self-sufficiency over dependence and need. Hauerwas believes that the inability of people with mental disabilities to hide their neediness makes others uncomfortable and that the diagnosis of "'retardation' might not 'exist' in a society which values cooperation more than competition and ambition." Hauerwas, however, refuses to reduce all disability to social perceptions; he asserts that people with disabilities have significant needs that must be acknowledged and accommodated. He also argues against the claim that suffering is only in the eye of the beholder (that we suffer only because we have mistaken ideals of what we really need to flourish and that all suffering has meaning if we just have the insight to discover it). But he also wonders whether "too often the suffering we wish to spare [children with disabilities] is the result of our unwillingness to change our lives so that those disabled might have a better life."

When reading Becker and Hauerwas, I am aware that OI is a very different disorder than Down syndrome or other cognitive disabilities. (Some people even wonder if it is problematic to discuss "disability" in general when there are such degrees of disability and when physical and intellectual disabilities, in particular, are so different from each other. I will address this question later in this chapter.) With both physical and mental disabilities, some suffering is rooted in societal response rather than intrinsic pain; as a teenager and young adult, I suffered much more from having a body that failed to meet cultural norms of beauty than from fractures and pain. But up until puberty, fractures and surgeries brought real and brutal suffering into my life and my family's life. Any day could be interrupted by an excruciating fracture, followed by harrowing hours in the emergency room, months in plaster casts, and the countless indignities that came with them—bedpans and extra-large Velcro-fastened underpants and being stealthily stalked by gaping, curious children in the department-store sock aisle. Having OI meant sitting on a plastic sled on a Cape Cod beach, my casted leg wrapped in a waterproof trash bag, and forfeiting my starring role in the fourth-grade puppet show because I broke my arm the night before. Rodding surgeries meant weeklong hospitalizations, burning pre-op injections in the buttocks that I dreaded more than the surgery itself, postoperative pain and nausea, blood-soaked plaster casts, and being left alone after visiting hours ended at 8:00 p.m. and my exhausted parents went home to care for their other two children.

So while I agree with Becker and Hauerwas that we must be cautious about equating neediness and genetic difference with suffering, I am also interested in finding out what else my faith has to say about suffering and whether it is ever reasonable for Christians to try to avoid a particular kind of suffering by using increasingly sophisticated medical, reproductive, and genetic technologies. In other words, what does God have to do with the snap of bone, the spirit- and body-withering days spent in plaster, the disappointments and exclusions that always took me by surprise when they really should not have? What does God have to say about my desire to spare my children these agonies?

Christian Perspectives on Suffering

In my ongoing research and conversations about God, suffering, and disability, I have come across three broad Christian narratives on the origins and meaning of suffering caused by illness, disability, and disease.

First is the idea that suffering is something God either proactively orchestrates (suffering as a fundamentally good thing that God gives for good reasons) or passively allows (God does not cause the suffering but allows it to happen to further some purpose) as part of a divine plan that humans cannot fully understand.

In the second common Christian narrative about suffering, God created humans as free to live an abundant life in full communion with God (Genesis 2–3). Once human beings failed to hold up their end of the bargain by trying to transcend the limits God put on them, a separation (sin) came between God and creation. As a result of this separation (the fall), the world does not work as God meant it to. People must engage in ceaseless labor to survive, women experience more pain in childbirth, people are separated from one another and from God, and bodies break and eventually die. As my friend Tina once said in an e-mail exchange, this narrative assumes that "our world is so fallen that even our cells don't act as God designed them."

A third approach specifically addresses genetic disorders and other suffering caused by occurrences in the natural world, such as natural disasters. A commenter to an online article I wrote insisted that "disability is disability, period," the result neither of God's intent nor the world's fallenness. God designed the world in all its glory and intricacy, but the same God-given laws that work for the good of the world and humans can also work against them. Genetic mutations are good and necessary because they ensure human adaptation and diversity. That some mutations have disabling or devastating effects is inevitable, just as the good gifts of rain and rivers that support humans, animals, and plants can also wipe out villages in catastrophic floods.

Until I dug deep into questions about the nature of suffering and disability in writing this book, I accepted the third approach. I thought questions of "Why?" and particularly "Why me?" were a waste of time and a reflection of a skewed self-centeredness that inflates the questioners' importance, implying that there must be some grand reason that they, in all their fabulousness, should have to suffer so. The idea that my OI is the result of an inevitable mishap in the intricate beauty of the genetic code seemed neat and simple; it allowed me to avoid tedious theological discussions that I generally find inaccessible and far removed from the daily experiences of actual people.

But in doing research for this book, I started to see two major problems with this approach to genetic anomalies. First, if I believe that with God all things are possible (Matthew 19:26; Mark 10:27)—and I do believe that—then it's a stretch to believe that God would create precise and intricate mechanisms for genetic diversity without also creating precise and intricate mechanisms for ensuring that major mistakes don't happen. Second, this approach fails to explain or satisfy my gut-level sense that bones breaking when a child sits down on the bathroom floor (or lungs filling up with mucus when they shouldn't, as in cystic fibrosis; or muscles wasting away, as in muscular dystrophy; or aortas bursting open with no warning, as in Marfan syndrome) are fundamentally bad things. Is "evil" too strong a word? I'm not sure. They are somehow a manifestation of the separation between what God intends and desires for humankind on the one hand, and on the other hand what humankind actually lives with, day after heartbreaking day. Ascribing such suffering to plain old genetic diversity feels inadequate.

In responding to the devastating Asian tsunami on December 26, 2004, Eastern Orthodox theologian David B. Hart argues against any attempt to rationalize, ascribe meaning to, or trumpet God's intent in human suffering: "Ours is, after all, a religion of salvation; our faith is in a God who has come to rescue His creation from the absurdity of sin and the emptiness of death, and so we are permitted to hate these things with a perfect hatred." Hart calls attempts to justify human misery on grounds that our suffering is necessary to reveal God's true nature "immeasurably . . . vile"; he goes on to ask which attributes of God the tragic deaths of children (and I would add, the painful disabilities of children) are meant to reveal: "Capricious cruelty, perhaps? Morbid indifference? A twisted sense of humor?" A thousand ancient knots in my chest undid themselves the moment I read this sentence: "Simply said, there is no more liberating knowledge given us by the gospel—and none in which we should find more comfort—than the knowledge that suffering and death, considered in themselves, have no ultimate meaning at all."

I have come to believe that illness, disability, and disease are neither fundamentally good things disguised as bad (thus not the intentional work of a loving God who works in mysterious ways) nor value-neutral manifestations of human diversity. I view suffering as a characteristic of life in a fallen world; illness, disability, and disease are, quite simply, the result of life in a world that does not work as God intended. I believe they are bad things and that we are allowed to name them as bad things. This does *not* mean, however, that we have license to try to fix what is wrong at all costs or that we can't learn valuable lessons, find meaning, and come to know God and ourselves better as a result of suffering. There is a huge difference between saying that my bone disorder was *intended* to reveal God's truth or teach me something I need to know and saying that my bone disorder *ended up* revealing God's truth or teaching me something I need to know. While I refuse to ascribe God's intent to disability, disease, and suffering, I acknowledge that they often provide life-changing opportunities for growth.

Disability, Identity, and Limitation

In early 2010 preliminary research showing that drug therapy could potentially improve cognitive function in people with Down syndrome lit up the blogosphere with discussion of whether, if it becomes possible to cure Down syndrome, we *should* cure Down syndrome. The question "Should Down syndrome be cured?" was actually quite premature. The research was done on mice, not humans, and evaluated a potential therapy, not a cure. Nevertheless it sparked fascinating discussions around the intersection between disability and identity.

A number of parents of children with Down syndrome spoke up, saying that their children's intellectual capacity, while affected by Down syndrome, is coupled with an openness, acceptance, and appreciation for life's goodness that actually gives these children an advantage in some ways. "Our children are happy and loving," these parents said. "They are not suffering greatly, and they live in a way that the rest of us should emulate, not try to fix." The parents worried that treatment to improve cognitive function was equivalent to altering the identity of people with Down syndrome. They argued that welcoming and accepting those with genetic differences just as they are, rather than trying to fix them, opens our eyes to the right of all human beings to live out their unique destinies and be recognized for their own strengths. I chimed in on the debate, arguing that genetic disorders, while certainly a manifestation of human diversity and a vehicle for both God's grace and human learning, are still, quite simply, an example of how the world is not as it should be.

Hauerwas defines suffering as something that "by its very nature . . . alienates us not only from one another but [also] from ourselves. . . . To suffer is to have our identity threatened physically, psychologically, and morally. Thus our suffering even makes us unsure of who we are." Hauerwas cautions that suffering is *not* to be equated with the limitations and neediness that are not only simply part of being human but also necessary if we are to live and love well. But suffering can lead to a real separation, in which we are alienated both within and without. Disability and illness foster separation—the sense that one's body is at war with itself, or as I have expressed it at times, that my body betrays me. Disability and illness prevent people from engaging in core human functions that connect us to each other and the world. Such separations cry out for healing.

In the discussions about the potential for curing Down syndrome, some people wondered if it is a mistake to discuss "disability" in general. An intellectual disability and a physical disability such as OI are so different, with such different sources and degrees of suffering, with such different physical and social manifestations. In some responses to my contribution to the debate, people tried to simplify my suffering, saying that of course bones that break so easily are painful and bad, of course you want and need healing, but that's nothing like the situation that people with Down syndrome live with, where their personalities and interaction with the world are so tied up with the effects of their extra chromosome. That response was accurate in a way—and it was also really, really wrong. Assuming that my experience with OI is merely physical, the supersized version of a cut requiring stitches or a seven-year-old's broken wrist, fails to acknowledge how intricately body, mind, and spirit are connected. It's not just that my broken bones led to physical scars, which led to social exclusion as well as concrete pain. It's also that having OI is as much a part of who I am as my being Caucasian, the daughter of my particular parents, a writer, and a mother. Because OI is such a part of who I am, if a cure were magically bestowed on me tomorrow, I would no doubt reel from dislocation and befuddlement as to who I am now that my bones are straight and strong.

I've already had a glimpse of this dislocation. Since early adolescence, I have walked around on legs that have a two-inch length difference. When I first started wearing shoes to partially correct that problem in my late thirties, I felt uncomfortable and awkward. I ended up with a stress fracture of my left tibia, which was unused to walking in the new (straighter, healthier, more normal) position. My old way of walking was so much a part of who I was, flaws and all, that my body rebelled against a healthier way of walking. I walked straighter, but I felt out of sync. The late disability activist Harriet McBryde Johnson, who had a neuromuscular disease, wrote that "at 15, I threw away the back brace [that straightened her crooked spine] and let my spine reshape itself into a deep twisty S-curve. Now my right side is two deep canyons. To keep myself upright, I lean forward, rest my rib cage on my lap, plant my elbows beside my knees. Since my backbone found its own natural shape, I've been entirely comfortable in my own skin." Her disability, entirely physical, was such a part of who she was that she felt more complete, more herself, when she let the disability have its way with her body. So just as it is impossible to completely separate disability and identity, it is not quite so easy to separate physical and mental disabilities. We cannot claim that physical disability affects only a piece of one's identity, while mental disability permeates one's identity. Any person who lives with disability or experiences healing will be forever changed in ways that incorporate both gain and loss.

The connections among genetic disorders, identity, and limitations are complex and do not allow for a cut-and-dried assessment of which ailments are appropriately eradicated via medical technology and which conditions require that we learn to live with and accept them. Although disability and identity are intricately connected, I believe that connection *in and of itself* does not provide an adequate argument against seeking out new medical technologies and treatments for genetic disorders. As I said in my contribution to the debate raised by potential new treatments for Down syndrome, "I want to be accepted as I am, but I'll take a cure too."

Life as Gift versus Life as Choice

My evolving understanding of disability and suffering has prompted me to conclude that the usual Christian responses to suffering, particularly the suffering of illness and disability, are a bunch of hooey. Platitudes—such as "God does not give you more than you can handle" or "Everything happens for a reason"—merely trivialize suffering, portraying God as an abusive headmaster who whips his unruly students because it will make them better people in the long run; such bromides mostly serve to appease the fear and discomfort that people feel in the face of another's profound suffering. Many people have not yet figured out that, when you are witnessing someone else's suffering, often the best thing is to say nothing at all beyond "I'm so sorry you are in pain" and simply to remain in relationship, offering what help you can—making a meal, taking on necessary chores, being willing to listen without comment or judgment. Cliché responses to suffering are often a misguided attempt to make sense of senseless circumstances, respond to pain for which no response is adequate, and fill awkward silences.

The Bible and our human experience attest to the power of suffering to transform people, increase their faith, reorder their priorities, and teach kingdom-of-God values (love, gratitude for life as it is given, acceptance) over cultural ones (beauty, accomplishment, wealth). Yet that transformation does not make suffering good in and of itself, nor does it necessarily follow that God orchestrates suffering for the purpose of transformation. Stanley Hauerwas claims that "the suggestion that all forms of suffering are capable of being given human meaning is destructive to the human project. . . . No 'meaning' can be derived from the Holocaust except that we must do everything to see that it does not happen again. Perhaps individuals can respond to natural disasters such as hurricanes and floods in a positive manner, but humanly we are right to view these other destructions as a scourge which we will neither accept nor try to explain in some positive sense." While my suffering with OI does not compare in scale or horror with the Holocaust or the 2010 Haitian earthquake, I also refuse to see the suffering of illness and disability—even when it transforms, even when it is tied up with identity—as good and meaningful in and of itself.

Experiencing OI has certainly transformed me. Being disabled and parenting a disabled child have fostered in me a conscious, daily gratitude—for the ability to feed my children when they are hungry, to sit next to a sunny window with a good book, or to be surprised by daffodil shoots poking up from the cold earth when gray piles of snow still litter the yard. Knowing how fractures can bring our plans and hopes clattering down in a great heap leads me to be laid back about many of the things that make contemporary American parents anxious. I do not worry about my kids eating Halloween candy or white flour; wearing mismatched clothes; spending free time reading on the couch or drawing with chalk on the driveway instead of going to soccer practice and ballet class; failing to finish their homework on occasion; developing an overbite from sucking their thumbs; coming inside on a summer evening covered by mosquito bites; watching TV every day; or eating dessert every night. If they are happy enough, healthy enough, and kind enough, then I am satisfied. Living with OI may be one factor that helps me sift through all this world's chaff to find the wheat. But if given a choice between having the wisdom that comes from disability on one hand, and on the other hand forgoing the disability and perhaps some of the wisdom as well, I'd choose the latter.

Of course, I didn't have a choice. As Hans Reinders has written, "Life is good as it is, not because we chose it, or would have chosen it had there been a choice, but simply because it is what it is." He defines "two rival conceptions of the human good; one that makes life's goodness dependent upon 'choice,' the other that makes life's goodness dependent upon 'gift.'" Until quite recently, human reproduction and our children's genetic makeup were mysteries beyond our control. In late twentieth-century America, widely available contraception and legalized abortion gave people some limited choices over when they would and would not have children, but they still had no control over what sort of child they would have when the time came. New technologies are changing that, and so a new ideal is creeping into our notion of what makes a good life. We can choose whether to transfer one or two or five embryos; whether to selectively reduce some of those embryos if too many implant; whether to weed out genes that cause OI, cystic fibrosis, Huntington's disease, and breast cancer; or whether to increase the odds of having a girl over a boy. With all these possibilities, we begin to feel that we must make the right choices to ensure the best life for our children.

But Reinders points out the futility of equating a good life with one over which we exercise choice. If you ask parents of children with severe disabilities whether they would choose to conceive that child if they knew about the disability ahead of time, both a "yes" and a "no" answer pose problems. If they say "yes," then they are somehow surrendering to the suffering their child endures, saying it doesn't matter, when they surely know it does matter. But if they say "no," then they are saying their child's life is not good, when they surely know it is good. The answer to this conundrum, Reinders says, is to sever the connection between choice and life's goodness, to recognize that "if my life were different from what it happens to be, then it would also be good."

Reinders's insistence that life is good, no matter what, uncovers another problem with theorizing that "everything happens for a reason" or "God won't give you more than you can handle." While people with disabilities certainly need to fight a tendency for others to see them as *less than* fully human, these platitudes actually portray people with disabilities as *more than* fully human. In a strange way, they imply that the lives of disabled people are *more* valuable than other lives; that people with disabilities and their families are stronger, wiser, and tougher than regular people; and that they, in the words of one online commenter writing specifically about Down syndrome, have a "straighter line to God." Women's magazines, primetime television shows, and local news spots are full of stories about people with disabilities who are extraordinary. As a child and teenager, I felt anxious and resentful every time I heard one of these stories. I would think, "What I want most is to be a regular person, to be like my friends, to be able to walk, to have boys look at me. But apparently more is expected." One often-used slogan in the OI community is "unbreakable spirit." I know its purpose is to separate the fragile body from the inner person, but honestly, my spirit has often been broken because I am a human being, not a superhero. The beliefs that everything happens for a reason, that God won't give you more than you can handle, or (the one I dislike most) that God chooses special families for special children are easily disproved by reality. When working at the OI Foundation, I came across a photo of a five-year-old with relatively mild OI whose parents kept him lying down in a wagon, in diapers, drinking from a bottle—tell me that God chose those "special" parents for that abused little boy. These assertions also imply that disabled children and their families are better, in some way more valuable, than everyone else, to be chosen by God for this honor. This is a problem if we accept Reinders's assertion that *every* life is *always* good, no matter whether the human being living that life is weak or strong, disabled or robust, petty or bighearted, cranky or joyful.

The Gift of Life, the Weight of Choice

I do believe that life is a gift. But the simple presence of new choices and the possibility of weeding out my OI gene, thus sparing my children (and their children) this particular brand of suffering, compelled me to at least explore the choices increasingly available even to people of modest means like us.

When we had been married for a little more than a year and were ready to think about children, Daniel and I briefly explored preimplantation genetic diagnosis (PGD). In PGD, a couple goes through a standard course of in vitro fertilization (IVF), whereby the woman's ovaries are stimulated with hormone injections, multiple mature eggs are removed and fertilized in the laboratory, then several fertilized eggs are transferred to the mother's uterus. In PGD, however, an additional step after fertilization tests the embryos for a specific genetic defect—in our case, my OI mutation—and only unaffected embryos are transferred. I underwent some very basic genetic testing, via a tiny circle of skin removed from my upper arm, that confirmed my OI diagnosis but failed to identify my specific mutation. Without that information, PGD was impossible. Eager to have a baby yet reluctant to delve further into a process that would be physically and emotionally exhausting, not to mention ethically and spiritually fraught, we decided to conceive on our own (a decision I will discuss more thoroughly in the next chapter). Leah was born on December 10, 1999.

We felt foolishly confident that Leah would not have OI. We made the rookie theological mistake of thinking that because we had declined reproductive technologies, God would honor our faith, our willingness to take risks, and reward us with a perfectly healthy baby. Those around us shared our confidence. When I was pregnant, I mentioned to my mother the possibility that we'd have an OI baby, and she responded, "But you're not going to have an OI baby." A nurse whom I saw regularly in the weeks before I gave birth said, "I have a gut feeling your baby is going to be fine."

We were all wrong. Leah was officially diagnosed at six weeks old, but I knew she had OI before that because of how loose she was—not a tight little bundle you could scoop up in one hand, like most newborns—and because of her strangely colored eyes and the way her long, thin fingers and toes looked just like mine. I was awaiting the genetic counselor's confirmation of my suspicions when, one Saturday morning, I called my obstetrician because of some particularly heavy postpartum bleeding. He assured me that the bleeding was normal and then said, "I assume you've heard from the genetic counselor." When I said I hadn't, he had no choice but to tell me what he knew, which was that Leah's OI test had come back positive.

One afternoon when she was two weeks old (before we learned of the diagnosis), I held Leah's tiny body against my breast and said to God, "Goddamn it, if you let her have this disease, then you'd damn well better take care of her." And God has taken care of her (I realize this is just in God's nature and probably not a direct result of my pathetic ultimatum, but saying it did make me feel a little better). She has certainly suffered, my little one. She has broken bones while walking across the living room floor. She has screamed in outrage at being poked with yet another IV needle. She has leaned her head on my chest and whimpered that it's not fair. Lying on the ground in terrible pain just after a new fracture, she has cried that she would rather die than break another bone. But she has been cared for by kind and humble physicians, prayed for by people whose faith and hope are things to behold, and blessed with gentle friends who never seemed to care that she had to scoot gingerly down the Slip 'n Slide instead of taking a running jump. A close friend in preschool once told her mother, "I want to have a child with fragile bones, just like

Leah." How can I accuse God of not caring for Leah when we have been given such extreme love and acceptance?

So I believe God has indeed cared for her well, has blessed her in a way that has made life not just bearable, but also joyous and full. We have never regretted our decision to have Leah in spite of the even odds that she would have OI. But we have certainly wished that she didn't have it.

That is a difficult sentiment to admit; honest acknowledgment of the grief, envy, rage, and even regret that raising a child with a disability can bring is rare among parents. We don't want people to misunderstand. Of course we love our children fiercely, of course it's not all drudgery and pain, of course we have learned more than we could have imagined about acceptance and gratitude for unexpected gifts. But it is still heartbreaking and exhausting to raise a child who is in pain, who can't do what other children do easily, who looks or acts different enough that a trip to the grocery store or a dinner out can quickly become tiresome, even ugly, when strangers ask probing questions or make assumptions.

Though I've read dozens of articles and books written by and about parents with disabled children over the years, I can recall only two instances where parents have admitted that sometimes the weight of their daily struggle to raise their children is too much. In one magazine article (I've long ago forgotten the source), a mother raising twins with significant disabilities from their premature birth recounted her children's daily routine of treatments, therapies, medications, and accommodations; then she remarked, "I love my children, but I hate my life." More recently I read Ayelet Waldman's *Bad Mother*, which includes an essay on Waldman's decision to abort a fetus with a chromosomal abnormality, despite her husband's desire to continue the pregnancy. The fetus's particular abnormality is relatively rare and not well studied. It could lead to significant disability or to hardly any disability at all, and it is impossible to know ahead of time which way things will go. Desperate for answers, Waldman found the home phone number of a physician who had written an article on the abnormality. Weeping, Waldman asked the doctor what she should do. The doctor apologized that "she could not give me a medical key to unlock my terrible puzzle. But, she said, she could talk to me as a parent. She told me that she had a son, a teenager now, who was mentally retarded. 'He's the light of my life,' she said. 'I love him desperately.' I listened, wondered if I could ever be such a self-abnegating mother. Such a *Good* Mother. 'But if I had to do it all over again,' [the doctor] continued, 'I would have an abortion.'"

I neither hate my life nor wish I had aborted Leah. But I am grateful to these mothers for their honesty.

When it comes to genetic disorders, OI—particularly the milder form that Leah and I have—is relatively manageable. I know that I should simply give thanks for that, for Leah, and for my own rich life. And I *am* grateful, every day. Even so, I hate that I have OI and I hate that Leah has it. There are reasons why parents wish and hope and pray for healthy babies, and those reasons go beyond cultural biases toward achievement and health. Quite simply, it is hard to care for a fragile child, a child for whom the most routine activities—walking in socks on a bare floor, speeding up to keep up with her class in the school hallway—are dangerous. And it is likewise hard to be that child. Whatever wisdom, gratitude, or kindness I have in me, and that Leah has in herself, have certainly been shaped by our experience with OI. But there are many wise, grateful, kind people who have never broken a bone in their lives, who have moved through life while experiencing plenty of disappointments and setbacks, but no major grief, ailment, or catastrophe.

If I get anything from contemplating the cross, it is that God redeems suffering, that God can bring something good from something terrible. But if it were up to me, I'd ask God to try to make me who he wants me to be without all the scars and aching joints. I would ask God to help Leah become a compassionate and faithful person without her needing to lie on the floor while screaming and sweating after a broken femur. If, as it seemed when Leah was small and so fragile, God was unable or unwilling to protect my children from the suffering of OI, then perhaps I needed to do it instead. When we began to think about having a second child, the wrenching decisions and stress around PGD that we had decided to avoid the first time around didn't seem quite so overwhelming. Perhaps, I thought, we should give PGD a second look.

Questions to Think About

1. What responses to or explanations for suffering have you come across in conversations or readings? What do you think of those perspectives?
2. Is there any value in suffering? Or is suffering always to be avoided and eliminated when possible?
3. What is the nature of suffering caused by illness and disability? Does suffering primarily come from physical pain and limitations, from cultural stigma and exclusion, or both?
4. How are Christian perspectives on human limitations different from or the same as cultural perspectives?

2

Setting Out

Desire, Vocation, and Choosing to Have Biological Children

We all have one, don't we? A first or greatest love, the one we thought was The One—until it turned out that, actually, he or she wasn't.

After college, I went to Washington, D.C., to work in an Episcopal social service agency and ended up staying in Washington for nine years. I joined the Potter's House Church—a tiny, ecumenical, social justice-minded church that met in a coffeehouse in the Adams Morgan neighborhood. At the Potter's House, I met Aaron.* I experienced something with Aaron that I'd never had before— an almost immediate, intense attraction that was (get this) *mutual*. In fact, he noticed me first. Shortly after we met, I returned home from an evening out, and my roommate announced that Aaron had stopped by. He and a friend were out for a bike ride and had bought some cheesecake. They came to my apartment to share it. This was stunning news.

I was in love with Aaron for nearly two years. We acted like we were dating—going out on weekends, cooking dinner together, talking regularly on the phone, meeting each other's families—but never so much as kissed, and we never really talked about what was happening between us. I didn't understand what the problem was, though I suspected it was probably me—crooked, broken me. Then Aaron started casually mentioning a woman he had known in college, who had just moved to Baltimore for medical school. After pretending for many months that this woman did not exist, I ended up on Aaron's

---

*Not his real name.

37

couch, telling him that I could not see him anymore. I would not be number two after this person who was staking some kind of claim on him. I would not play the role of the faithful friend when I knew that there was more than friendship between us. I accused him of not being able to see beyond my physical imperfections.

In defending himself, Aaron told me that he had thought a lot about whether I was the woman he wanted to marry. He meant to prove that my physical problems did not prevent him from seeing me as a potential mate. Instead he proved to me what a fool I had been. I had been so certain that I was undesirable that I waited until it was too late to name our obvious and mutual attraction to each other. As those two years went by with me and Aaron intensely connected to each other but still "just friends," I reasoned—wrongly, as it turned out—that I was reading something into this relationship that was not there. That, after all, had been the story of my love life up until then.

Aaron promised to teach me to ride a bike, something I had never done in my fragile childhood. I pictured us on top of a grassy hill, with the spring breeze against our cheeks like a kiss, and me on a red bike, flying down that hill. I imagined him watching, stretching his arms up to the sky, hands open, yelling, "Yes! That's it! Yes!" I imagined the sensation of grass below me, with bits of yellow as the dandelions flew by. No effort. No fear. Just movement. But Aaron never did anything so carefree as to stretch his hands up to catch the spring breeze, and he never said anything so clear as "Yes" to me. But then again, I never asked him to give me a clear answer until it was too late. It was October when I told Aaron and promised myself that I would not ever be the second choice in a man's life again. The following summer, he married the med student.

The scars on my legs were ugly but painless; the scars on my heart from years of watching the men I loved pair up with other women—usually tall, graceful, athletic women—oozed quietly, flaring up painfully every time I saw a girlfriend's engagement ring or bought a baby gift. I prayed, asking God to ease the hurt, to help me accept the life I was given, to focus on loving God and being the person I was supposed to be. During my years in D.C., the problem was that I became increasingly sure that my desires for a mate and children were more than just innate biological yearnings, more than my embracing of society's expectations. I became sure that God was calling me to partnership and parenthood as a vital piece of my vocation. I was confused: why would God call me to this when clearly the plan was not going well? And then I was angry: why would God give me this certainty of my call but never give me the means by which to fulfill it?

The Potter's House Church in D.C. was part of the larger Church of the Saviour—a church with the unusual distinction of taking both Jesus and social justice seriously. The church's founders, Gordon and Mary Cosby, frequently spoke about "call" and how to discern it. Gordon's most basic advice was to think on your heart's desire, for in that you would find the roots of your calling. The Church of the Saviour attracts the type of people who carry the weight of the world on their shoulders and do big things for Jesus. One woman dreamed of the Church of the Saviour's headquarters building (though she had never seen it and knew nothing of the church) and moved from Topeka to D.C. when she discovered that the building in her dreams was just off Dupont Circle. To provide medical services for the poor, another church member had left his life as a family physician in the rural Midwest, bringing his young family to Washington. Others moved out of their comfortable suburban homes to live in group homes for people with mental disabilities, chose to forgo health insurance as long as there were Americans who had no choice but to live without it, or raised families in D.C.'s toughest neighborhoods though they had the resources to live elsewhere. In this environment, I was dismayed when, time and again, I concluded that my heart's desire was to bear children. This could not possibly be right. But I could not escape it. During the most mundane moments at work or at home, I frequently had the sensation that I was forgetting something important. Then I would remember—"Oh, it's the *baby*. That's what I'm forgetting"—as if God had written, "Have the baby," on my life-long to-do list.

I was embarrassed by the mundane nature of this call among so many Christian overachievers. *Yes, God is calling me to wipe pureed plums off some kid's chin while the rest of you are saving the world.* At the same time I was terrified of the possible outcome of having a baby. A Potter's House member gave a sermon once in which he said that faith is doing something that you believe God is calling you to do, knowing that there is no way you can do it without God's help. He asked us to think about what task in our lives might fit that description. I could answer immediately: my impossible task, the thing I could not possibly do with my own meager resources, was to have a child who inherited OI.

I accused God of teasing me with this call to marriage and motherhood, given that I was past my twenty-fifth birthday and seemed to have "Just Friends" stamped indelibly on my forehead. The end of my relationship with Aaron sealed the deal. This was it. When even the guy who claimed to have given considerable thought to whether I was marriage material decided the answer was "no" without actually *dating* me while he figured it out (much less telling me that he was figuring it out), I knew there was simply no hope.

But then I did find a mate, right in my tiny little church, where attendance on a good day topped out at around forty people, many of them retirees with grown children—not a great place for meeting single men.

Daniel and I each had our vision of the right partner, and neither of us fit the other's. Daniel is an outdoorsman and gravitated toward well-toned hiker-type women. So much for me. Despite all the evidence that I wasn't making the best choices in my objects of affection, I always fell for outgoing activists—men whose time and talents were in demand, men whose attention made me feel special because they had an endless supply of willing companions. Daniel was smart and ambitious yet also solitary and awkward.

Several weeks after we met, a good friend asked if I had any romantic interest in Daniel. It had, quite frankly, never crossed my mind. My friend said that was good because she thought Daniel and my roommate would make a good couple. She was right—sort of. Daniel and my roommate dated for a year, then became engaged, but she eventually broke off the engagement. Two months later, Daniel went on a solo backpacking trip to the Sierra Nevadas, where he seriously considered whether he should throw himself off a cliff. He decided he should not. While he was gone, I realized that I really missed him. He missed me too; I was the first person he called when he came down from the mountains, ready to rebuild his shattered life.

Daniel and I never had a great romance; we knew each other so well by the time we started dating that we had none of that fluttery excitement of believing we had finally found the Perfect One. He knew I could not go backpacking with him in the Grand Tetons, as my roommate had. I knew he was struggling to figure out who he was and what he wanted and that he might decide, after the dust settled, what he wanted was not me. At one point, when I felt that Daniel might just be keeping me around for comfort during a hard time, I told him my vow that I would never again be number two behind any other woman (in this case, the idealized memory of his ex-fiancée) and broke up with him. Four days later he showed up at my door with red roses and chocolate and asked for another chance. I gave it to him. We were married two and a half years later.

It would be romantic to write that Daniel never thought twice about my having OI, but it would also be a lie. He never envisioned being married to a person with a disability—who does?—and marrying this crooked, stumbling person required him to embrace a new vision of what his life would be. Daniel and I both wanted children. While having a child with OI terrified me because I knew exactly what that meant, it terrified Daniel because he had no idea what it meant. By the time he met me, I was physically independent. He had never seen me in plaster or waited with me in the ER to get a fracture treated.

Before we learned about PGD, we saw only two choices for having biological children: We could either conceive a child with a 50 percent chance of inheriting OI or use egg donation to ensure our child's healthy bones. When we first heard of PGD, it felt like a crack opened in a door that I had been sure was locked tight. Like egg donation, PGD would be expensive, and the odds of conception and a successful pregnancy would be low—but at least our child would be genetically related to both of us.

Shortly after our marriage, we had some initial testing done to try to identify my OI mutation. Hundreds of different genetic mutations cause OI; many of them are located on a particular chromosome, but some are located elsewhere, and some mutations may be unique to a particular family. Locating a particular OI mutation can be tricky, and the mutation must be identified before PGD becomes possible. Otherwise the scientists who are testing the embryos have no idea what to look for. As we waited for the test results, I began to realize that PGD, while more appealing than some of our other choices, would not be easy. It would be expensive, physically demanding, and likely unsuccessful. Beyond that, I wasn't sure it was a good decision, morally or emotionally. This tinkering with human life was worrisome. And that old defiance—my insistence on behaving as if nothing was wrong with me and daring people and circumstances to tell me differently—made me want to just make a baby, all by ourselves, and then see what happened next.

The initial testing confirmed my OI diagnosis but was unable to locate my mutation, making PGD impossible without further, more expensive testing. I was relieved at the testing failure, for it spared us an agonizing decision. Time and circumstance softened the hard edges of our fear, and when we decided to conceive on our own, I was pregnant within a few months. Leah was born a year after we moved from D.C. to Connecticut, to the town where I had grown up and where Daniel found his first job after graduate school, as a medical librarian at a university.

As Leah grew from a sedentary baby and toddler to a walking and breaking preschooler, and as we were increasingly batted around by the cruel winds of her OI, we again faced some choices. We could have just one child. We could adopt a baby. We could conceive another baby naturally and see how the odds came out this time, knowing that we could easily end up with two fragile children. Or, for a price, we could revisit the technologies available to us and thus ensure that our second baby would not have OI.

We honestly never really considered the first option—having an only child. I would like to cloak this decision in a righteous mantle, invoking my call to motherhood. But though I believe that call to be authentic, I also know that many of the reasons we wanted more than one child were purely human. Daniel had suffered through the unexpected deaths of his father from cancer and two of his brothers from suicide. His college mentor, a Baptist minister, had lost his only son in a fire when the boy was a young adult. We wanted more children for one of the oldest reasons there is: we were too aware of the potential, even in our well-nourished and technologically advanced society, that we could lose our one and only and be forever childless. Beyond that dark fear, there were more banal reasons: Relationships among siblings can be some of the most enduring our children will ever have. When we envisioned our married life, we pictured a back

seat full of kids, all the chairs around our kitchen table full at sup-
pertime, more than one face peeking through the stair banisters on
Christmas morning.

I also craved the physical challenge of bearing more children.
Even before getting pregnant with Leah, I suspected that my body—
so imperfect and incapable in many ways—would prove capable of
making and nurturing babies. I had no trouble becoming pregnant
and no pregnancy complications, other than Leah's breech presenta-
tion, which meant that she was delivered by C-section. I loved being
pregnant, having a newborn, and breast-feeding. I bounced back
from my C-section more easily than many friends recovered from
their vaginal births. By the time Leah was one week old, I was walking her around the block in her stroller. My body seemed to confirm
that bearing children was something I was made to do.

People tend to offer adoption as an obvious solution to the problems of infertility or family history of genetic disease. I have read
dozens of articles, books, and blog posts about people who have used
reproductive technologies, from IVF to surrogacy, to have children
who are biologically related to at least one parent or who are free of
particular genetic disorders. Inevitably a number of dismayed readers wonder why these couples didn't just adopt a child who needs
parents. These responses imply that anyone who chooses assisted
reproduction over adoption is selfish. Though I understand some of
what these outraged readers are feeling—I am not always sympathetic to people who go to extreme lengths to have biological children—I also want to tell them, "It's just not that simple."

The whole reason Daniel and I would choose adoption over natural conception would be to avoid having another child with a disability. We were not looking to adopt a special-needs child because
that was what we were trying to avoid in the first place. Adopting a
healthy child would cost as much as (if not more than) PGD, and be
as long and arduous a process in its own way. Daniel and I were well
aware of the potential genetic strikes against any biological children
we would have—not only my OI but also the addiction and depression that were part of his family history. These risks were frightening enough, but taking on the unknown genetic legacy of an adopted
child was more so. Our tepid consideration of adoption was rooted in
emotion and history, not ethics or faith. We preferred to grapple with

known risks rather than unknown. (Later in this chapter I address the complexities of adoption further. Daniel and I also had some other reasons, rooted in family history, that made us reluctant to pursue adoption. Explaining those reasons would require me to tell stories that are not only mine to tell.)

Our reasons for wanting another biological child sound selfish because they were. One of the hardest things about exploring assisted reproduction is having to face, and claim, these selfish desires. Most people who want to have babies don't have to justify why. The drive to have biological children is wired into us. Overcoming that drive and accepting that one's path to parenthood may lie elsewhere is one of the hardest things we can ask human beings to do. People with genetic disease or infertility are asked to walk down roads that most parents never even glance at on the map.

When we first decided to look into PGD once again, Leah was not yet two years old and, though significantly delayed in motor skills, had not yet broken a bone. But we had begun to see what OI could do to her spirit, and to ours. One July day, Leah and I were at a friend's house for one of our weekly playgroup gatherings. This group of mothers and toddlers had formed the year before, when we all signed up for an informal class for new parents at a local community center. When the class ended, we continued to meet at each other's homes every week. On this day the summer weather was perfect—warm, sunny, and dry, with a breeze. We congregated on the back porch of our friend's home. For the other mothers and toddlers, the outdoors meant freedom. The kids could run around in the fenced yard, and the moms could sit on the porch with their coffee cups and bagels, with no worries about kids falling down stairs or smearing cream cheese on the couch. For me and Leah, the outdoors spelled limitation. Leah, at eighteen months old, could only scoot on her bottom to get around. The yard had a large hill, so I had to watch constantly to make sure Leah didn't tumble down it. She wanted to use one of the abundant riding toys but could not get up onto the seat herself and needed me by her side to make sure she didn't fall off or go rolling willy-nilly down the hill. While my friends chatted on the porch, I crouched by Leah's side, tense and frustrated.

Even as toddlers, the kids in this group were gentle and bighearted. None of them were pushers, hitters, or biters. When Leah grew a little older and started having fractures, the host mothers made a point of having sedentary activities available at our weekly playgroups, such as Play-Doh to squish or cookies to frost. But on that gorgeous July day, the rest of the kids wanted to run and jump, and so Leah was left alone, unable to join in, needing my help for the simplest actions. She articulated her frustration the only way she knew how, by becoming whiny, clingy, and demanding. I felt like OI was pulling us down into the muck, keeping us from the fluid freedom that such a summer day promises. So we went home. I felt sadder that day than I had any day since Leah was diagnosed.

A month later Daniel and I arrived at the Center for Advanced Reproductive Services at the University of Connecticut Health Center (hereafter called the Center). We met with one of the head doctors, a young, soft-spoken physician who would occasionally surprise me with some bit of dry humor or odd story. I learned from him, for example, that some of the hormones initially used for fertility treatment were harvested from the urine of a bunch of Italian nuns. Our first step, he told us, was to see if my OI mutation could be identified through more extensive DNA testing. Daniel, Leah, and I sent our blood samples to a Seattle lab that specializes in collagen disorders, and we waited. We had been told it would take six months. Six months passed, and there was no word. Our genetic counselor called the lab and learned that they were having a hard time finding the mutation. I felt both disappointed and relieved. If they absolutely could not locate my mutation, then once again we would not have to decide whether to try PGD. It would be decided for us. Then one day in March 2002, the counselor called and told us that, on the brink of giving up, the lab had decided to try a different technique and had found my mutation. We could try PGD if we wanted to and if we could pay for it.

Why People Want Children

When Leah was a baby, my father once said to me, "Having kids is great, except that they ruin your life." He was joking, in a serious sort of way. Children cost money, require attention day and night, and are self-centered. Their nonstop needs interfere with just about any effort parents make to control their finances, homes, health, and schedules. At a moment's notice, parents must be willing to clean up a soiled bed, go to the emergency room, cancel long-anticipated plans, and be wide awake at 3:00 a.m.

Given the unrelenting labor of raising children, why do people want them so badly? Most would agree that the desire for biological children is innate, although science, psychology, sociology, and religion offer different explanations for why that is. Evolutionary science explains that we are hardwired to propagate our genes, so that attracting a mate, conceiving children genetically related to both the male and female partners, and keeping those children alive until *they* are old enough to procreate—these become primary goals of adulthood. Psychosocial reasons for childbearing include establishing one's identity as a parent, thereby claiming the rights, responsibilities, and respect given to parents in one's society; a desire to carry on a family name, perpetuate bloodlines, or preserve one's culture; and a perception that one's well-being or happiness will be enhanced by childbearing.

Studies have shown both that women "reflect more intensely on their desire for children than men" and that women "are to a larger extent guided to motherhood than men to fatherhood" due to their bodily participation in gestation and childbirth, their role as primary caregivers of young children in most cultures, and societal expectations. Women often perceive motherhood as adding value to their lives in some way; they may live in cultures that celebrate mothers or expect women to become mothers, and they may perceive their motherhood role not only as nurturing children, but also as bringing together family members and neighbors in a web of relationships. There is some disagreement over whether women's desire for children is imposed upon them by culture or whether culture reinforces an intrinsic want. But it is clear that many women express a strong desire for children.

Although my experience of physical disability enhanced my eagerness to bear children, I am certainly not alone in experiencing a visceral longing for physical participation in pregnancy and birth—a longing that contributes significantly to the demand for reproductive technology that allows infertile women (or those married to infertile men) to gestate and birth babies. Pregnancy and birth are two of the most intimate and powerful human activities. No one but a biological mother knows how it feels to have a baby's foot tickle her from the inside. Pregnancy both connects women to the outside world in ways they rarely experience otherwise (complete strangers, for example, become interested in and solicitous of a pregnant woman whom they would pass by without a thought under different circumstances) and isolates women in a self-contained interior world. Ethicist Christine Gudorf recalls reading an article by the novelist Mary Gordon, "who spoke of being heavy with child, immersed in a shrunken, private world replete with content, preoccupied with the reality of her own body and the life within it, and resistant to reading the newspaper to check out the rest of the world." Women tell and retell their birthing stories because there are few human experiences as transforming as starting a day with a baby inside you and ending it with a baby in your arms. Gudorf believes that some women can even develop an addiction to pregnancy and lactation. Babies provide "easy intimacy" and offer to mothers "power to structure the relationship, power to interpret the baby's needs and wants, and the awesome power of being personally necessary to the very existence of the child."

But even when women's propensity toward childbearing does not qualify as addiction, there is no doubt that many women and men experience their desire for children as instinctive and potent, enhanced by cultural expectations but not rooted in them. Journalist Liza Mundy believes that "most of all, what reproductive science has done . . . is remind us that having children and loving children is an unstoppable urge; that humans, or many humans, have an overpowering need to have—to be—a family."

For those who believe in God, then, it makes sense to conclude that God has created us to want and to have babies. If our desire for children comes from God, then how are Christians to view decisions to have or not have children, particularly given the choices available to help people have babies even when they face challenges to natural conception?

Children as Vocation, Children as Choice

In the beginning, God told human beings to "be fruitful and multiply" (Genesis 1:28 NRSV). Likewise, after the flood, God commanded Noah to "be fruitful and increase in number; multiply on the earth and increase upon it" (Genesis 9:7 NIV). Having children is one of the 613 *mitzvot* (rules or commandments) that observant Jews live by. Childbearing is so central to traditional Judaism that even Orthodox Jewish authorities have many fewer reservations about reproductive technology than their counterparts in Christian churches. Such technology is often viewed as a tool to help Jews fulfill God's mandate by conceiving healthy children in spite of infertility or a family history of genetic disease, especially given that a number of recessive genetic disorders disproportionately affect people of Ashkenazi Jewish genetic background.

Although Christians share an allegiance to the same God and Hebrew Scriptures as Jews, they perceive the mandate to "be fruitful and multiply" in light of Jesus Christ's birth, death, and resurrection. Martin Luther interpreted God's mandate to procreate as a reflection on how God made us. Luther "believed that it [the command to be fruitful and multiply] was more than a simple command to which we respond in rational assent. Rather, he understood it to speak of a very basic truth about human nature. God has created us in such a way that we *have* to multiply. The sexual appetite and instinctive drives to reproduce are a gift from God."

But the God-given desire to reproduce does not mean that every Christian is obligated to reproduce. Christian theologians have argued that parenthood is a vocation, a response to God's call. Parenthood is not merely a peripheral activity that we engage in (or not) solely in response to our preferences, biology, or cultural expectations. If parenthood is a vocation, then an innate desire to have babies does not necessarily mean we should have them; conversely, those who feel no great desire for children are not necessarily justified in avoiding parenthood. Rather, when deciding whether we should become parents, we should look deeper than our innate desire for children and examine the particular gifts God has given us and the ways God is calling us to live out our faith.

Understanding procreation as a vocation, however, is not the same as understanding procreation as a choice—an important distinction in our modern culture, in which "choice" is central to discussions of reproductive ethics and rights. By treating parenthood as something one does or doesn't do based solely on personal choice or preference, we begin to see children as products we procure on our own terms. We also come to value children who are wanted, planned, and expected (those who are chosen) more than those who are not. Anglican cleric Anna Poulson makes this important distinction: "Regarding having children as a vocation is rather different than regarding them as a choice, yet Christians often confuse the two. . . . Vocation is a gift to us from God, whereas choice is generated by my own volition. Furthermore, vocations given by God are always faithful to and limited by his own designs; some options just aren't on the menu." Understanding parenthood as a vocation rather than a choice means that Christians may not exercise their "right" to bear children at all costs. This constraint becomes more meaningful, and perhaps more burdensome, in our technologically advanced culture, which offers myriad ways for people to overcome limitations on natural conception.

Understanding parenthood as a vocation also means that Christians must consider bearing and rearing children within the context of God's intentions for marriage. In traditional Christian theology, sexual intercourse and procreation are God-given and necessary components of marriage. That sex and procreation were designed to go together may seem to be an obvious fact, not even worth mentioning, except when one considers what happens when sex and procreation are separated, as they are in assisted reproduction. The necessary relationship between procreation and sexual intercourse forms the basis for the Roman Catholic Church's opposition to all forms of assisted reproduction—from artificial insemination with the husband's sperm, to donor sperm and eggs, IVF, PGD, and surrogacy—and reveals the difference between procreation and reproduction.

Procreation versus Reproduction

Christian bioethicist Gilbert Meilaender, along with other theologians and ethicists, points out the significant difference between "procreation" (a new human life arising from the love between a man and a woman) and "reproduction" (the technical process of egg and sperm joining to create a baby). This distinction is not simply two ways of looking at the same process; instead, it illustrates two essentially different perspectives on sex, marriage, and bearing children. Meilaender explains how the procreative view points us toward God: "That the sexual union of a man and a woman is naturally ordered toward the birth of children is, in itself, simple biological fact, but we may see in that fact a lesson to be learned. . . . A child who is thus begotten, not made, embodies the union of his father and mother. They have not simply reproduced themselves, nor are they merely a cause of which the child is an effect. Rather, the power of their mutual love has given rise to another. . . . Their love-giving has been life-giving; it is truly *pro*creation." Of assisted reproduction, which separates the process of uniting sperm and egg from the act of love, Meilaender asserts, "In our world there are countless ways to 'have' a child, but the fact that the end 'product' is the same does not mean that we have *done* the same thing." Theologians and ethicists, like Meilaender, worry that when we use technology to create babies, we give precedence to our will and our wants, transforming children from gifts that arise directly from the love between a man and a woman to products that we pay clinicians to produce on our behalf.

The Roman Catholic Church's opposition to all forms of assisted reproduction centers on these concerns about the proper relationship among sex, procreation, and marriage. Catholic doctrine asserts that marriage has two necessary and complementary purposes: unitive (two people becoming one flesh) and procreative (producing children). These purposes cannot be separated. Sex should not occur without the potential for procreation (hence the objection to artificial contraception), and procreation should not occur without sex (hence the objection to any method of assisted reproduction in which conception occurs independently of intercourse). The potential commodification of children that arises from the separation of sex and procreation is also a major concern, as is the Catholic Church's belief that from the moment of conception, embryos are fully human, with all the rights of a human being and created in God's image.

Many Protestant churches and theologians share the Catholic Church's concerns with the transformation of children from gifts to commodities, the separation of the reproductive process from the sexual union of parents, and the treatment of embryos. But Protestants tend to allow more leeway in the use of contraception and assisted reproduction, believing that it is reasonable for people to constrain natural processes under some circumstances. In general, mainline Protestant churches accept contraception and limited use of assisted reproductive technology, arguing that the link between sex and procreation, while important, manifests itself in the context of a lifelong marriage relationship, not just in discrete acts of sexual intercourse. In other words, couples can remain open to God's design for new life to arise from their sexual union while also using contraception to limit family size and time pregnancies, and using reproductive technology, within limits, to overcome infertility or address a family history of significant genetic conditions. However, assisted reproduction techniques that compromise the exclusive marriage relationship by allowing for conception outside of marriage or bringing third parties into the process (such as donor eggs, donor sperm, and surrogacy) raise concerns among many Protestants.

I confess that theological discussions of God's intentions for sex, procreation, and marriage sometimes make my eyes glaze over. These discussions can become overly theoretical, concerned more with the ideal than the real. Take contraception, for example. It sounds lovely for couples to be open to whatever children arise from their union. I have close friends who speak eloquently of how the Catholic practice of natural family planning (NFP) has enriched their marriage. In NFP, couples who wish to temporarily avoid conception, because they want to time their pregnancies or limit family size, abstain from intercourse during the wife's fertile days, which she identifies through detailed, consistent observation of body temperature and cervical mucus. Those who espouse NFP say that it not only works as well as artificial contraception (when done correctly, which requires knowledge and commitment), but it also enhances marital intimacy and interdependence by teaching couples to control their sexual urges in service to a greater goal.

Yet I am not convinced that controlling one's fertility through timed intercourse is morally superior to controlling one's fertility through contraceptive use. NFP proponents argue that their method honors the God-given fertility cycle, while artificial contraception manipulates it. But although the method may be different, the intent—controlling one's fertility to bring it in line with one's preferences—is not. And though I understand the benefit of being open to God's plans for my family, God is not the one who has to nurse the baby (whose poopy diaper is leaking onto his third outfit of the day), while singing Barney songs with an overtired toddler to keep her from melting down before dinner, quizzing an older child on her spelling words, and watching the pasta pot to make sure it doesn't boil over. Parental time, attention, and resources are limited, and in most families and cultures, mothers in particular make enormous sacrifices of time, energy, physical and mental health, and economic security. Even sacrifices taken on willingly and joyfully can take a toll. While I am grateful for my body's miraculous capability to carry and nurture children, I also see contraception as a tool for women to avoid the less savory, sometimes dangerous, results of unlimited childbearing, from fatigue to fistulas—as a tool that, unlike NFP, does not require women to shoulder yet another task (monitoring her fertility cycle) in service to her family. Perhaps in a better world, where all parents have access to the community support, financial resources, and health care they need to care for themselves and their children, we can do away with contraception. In the world as it is, however, I'll hang on to my birth control.

And yet I have come to understand that separating sex and procreation has concrete consequences. Many dystopian novels—stories of future worlds in which essential human values have been lost—are set in societies where sexual intercourse and reproduction occur independently of each other. In Aldous Huxley's *Brave New World*, for example, sex is encouraged as a social activity, even for the young, but children are manufactured in a process designed for efficiency and the propagation of traits that support a consumer society. Lois Lowry's young adult novel *The Giver* portrays a culture in which women possessing certain qualities (a robust body and relatively low intelligence) are housed separately from everyone else and given the job of bearing children. The children are then matched with parents and raised in what appear to be traditional nuclear families—except that parents have no biological ties to the children they raise, and infants who do not meet cultural standards are euthanized (even for problems as basic as fussiness or difficulty in sleeping through the night). As these and other dystopian novels illustrate, theologians are not the only ones who recognize the potential dangers of separating sex from procreation.

While the family structures in *The Giver* are troubling, in the real world, parents' raising biologically unrelated children is often a good thing. Adoption provides permanent families for children who might otherwise grow up in orphanages, foster care, or on the street. Given the complex ethical and theological questions raised by reproductive technology, adoption seems a simple, straightforward, and morally unambiguous choice for prospective parents. The common question put to people going to great lengths to have biological children— "Why don't you just adopt?"—is understandable. But the question mistakenly assumes that adoption is both easier than and morally superior to the use of reproductive technology.

"Why Don't You Just Adopt?"

My preferred answer to the question "Why don't you just adopt?" is "Why don't *you*?" Those who ask this question often have biological children or don't have any children at all. When adoptive parents chime in on debates over the merits of adoption versus the use of reproductive technology, they tend to say that, while adoption is a wonderful choice that they are glad they made, adoption is not easy and is not for everyone. As Catholic ethicist Maura A. Ryan has observed, "The call to adoption is almost always applied selectively. A case can be made that all Christian couples, all Christian families, have obligations to take the needs of abandoned, neglected, or endangered children into account in making procreative decisions. . . . However, as a practical matter, it is only infertile persons who are expected to assume such a duty. Fertile persons can reproduce at will, and they are not expected to match their procreative desires with the needs of the nation or of the world."

Adoption is a child-loving, life-affirming choice for creating a family. It is a choice that many people who struggle with infertility or carry specific genetic risks eventually make. For some moms and dads, it is even the first choice for becoming parents. The question "Why don't you just adopt?" implies that adoption is the best, easiest, most loving, least selfish choice for those struggling with biological parenthood. But there are several valid, thoughtful, and honest reasons why some people choose not to adopt children.

Adoption is not simple. As with assisted reproduction, adoption can be a complex and emotionally fraught process. In both cases, prospective parents confront questions and assumptions—about why they want children and how they will behave as parents—that those who conceive naturally do not. No one responds to a couple's pregnancy announcement by asking, "Why is biological parenthood so important to you?" No one did a home study of me and Daniel before we brought Leah home from the hospital.

Adoptive parents go through a great deal of scrutiny and uncertainty: Will a birth mother like us enough to pick us to adopt her baby? Will she change her mind? Will our child someday want to find the birth parents, and how will that affect our relationship? Will we have to field questions about why our child looks so different from us every time we go to the playground? All parents live with uncertainty, but adoptive parents have to confront and accept a great deal of uncertainty up front.

Adoption can be expensive. Journalist Liza Mundy discusses research showing that "there have never been enough adoptable children in the United States to meet the demand of infertile couples. Even so, the supply used to be larger than it is now, and adopting them used to be, for better or worse, more informal and streamlined."

A shortage of U.S. children available for adoption has fueled two trends: (1) the increasing use of assisted reproduction and (2) a higher number of adoptions from other countries. International adoptions, as well as private domestic adoptions, can cost tens of thousands of dollars, the equivalent of several IVF cycles. Especially for couples who have already spent thousands on unsuccessful fertility treatments, the cost of adopting can be prohibitive. Although adopting through state agencies can be less expensive, the pool of healthy infants is small. Some parents-to-be are eager to adopt an older child or one with special needs, but some are not.

Needy children are not always adoptable children. Read a newspaper on any given day, and it is obvious that there is no shortage of needy children. But that does not automatically translate into an abundance of adoptable children. Theologian Paul Lauritzen identifies a "myth of unwanted children," writing that "even to talk about 'unwanted children' may be misleading in situations where a woman is relinquishing a child not because she is *unwilling* to care for her child, but because she is *unable* to do so. . . . To speak about 'unwanted children' is to fail to take seriously what is perhaps the most compelling reason women relinquish children, namely, poverty."

It is tempting to think that adoption is an appropriate way to help children who are poor but not necessarily unwanted. This dynamic was apparent in the spiked interest in adoption of Haitian children in the aftermath of the January 2010 earthquake. News coverage of the Haitian orphanage and adoption system illustrates the moral complexity of adopting children from poor countries. First, some experts point out that the last thing children traumatized by the earthquake needed was to travel to an unfamiliar place with adoptive parents, leaving behind their extended families and familiar communities. Their families might be poor and struggling, but even poor children are attached to their families and birthplaces. Second, it turned out that many children in Haitian orphanages actually had living parents, who voluntarily relinquished their children because they felt unable to care for them amid Haiti's poverty and chaos, even before the devastating earthquake. The blurry line between "I don't want my child" and "I can't care for my child" raises some moral questions. There is potential for exploitation in a system in which desperate parents surrender their children and better-off parents are looking for children to adopt. This is *not* to say that adoption is necessarily exploitative, but neither is adoption a clear win-win solution for needy children and people who long to become parents.

Observers are often too quick to judge adoption as selfless and biological parenthood as selfish. As I discussed earlier in this chapter, for many people the desire to have biological children is compelling and innate. Those who dismiss the desire for biological children as selfish while holding up adoption as selfless diminish the powerful forces—biology, emotions, circumstances, vocation—that influence people's decisions about whether and how to create a family.

Adoption is one way to become a parent, not an act of selfless heroism. One friend, the mother of two sons through adoption, admits that it bothers her when people say her boys are "lucky" or that she and her husband are "heroes" for adopting them. From her perspective, "All we did was create a family!" People pursue parenthood for a whole variety of reasons, conscious and unconscious, selfish and noble. Good parenting requires a large dose of selflessness, whether one's children are adopted or biological. And for Christians, the idea of parenthood as a vocation means that decisions about how to build a family need to be considered in light of our faith and our perceptions of where God is leading us. My friend who adopted two boys did so not because she was infertile, but because she and her husband sensed that God was leading them toward adoption.

Adoption involves loss. When I wrote a short article criticizing the question "Why don't you just adopt?" for *Christianity Today*, I worried that adoptive parents or adults who had been adopted as children would assume that I was criticizing adoption itself, rather than the question I find so problematic. To the contrary, I received several comments from adoptive parents who were grateful for the article precisely because they knew well the losses inherent to adoption. One commenter mentioned that her adopted niece lives with a "primal wound" as a result of being separated from her birth parents, despite having a wonderful adoptive family whom she loves. Another adoptive parent said: "While adoption is a positive experience for many adoptive families, others struggle with their decision. This includes the potential for attachment issues, as well as the need to address the child's losses associated with adoption. These often include the loss of birth relatives who are no longer part of their life, and even the simple connection of looking like your relatives." Paul Lauritzen put it succinctly: "We must face the fact that there are human costs to adoption and that every adoption involves loss."

Daniel and I were lucky. While OI gave us plenty of difficult decisions to make when it came to childbearing, we had no trouble in conceiving. If we had, could we have overcome our deep desire to have biological children? Probably. Eventually. But we would have had to reach that point in our own way, allowing time to grieve the experience of bearing biological children and adjusting our vision of how our life with children would come about. We would not have been convinced by someone asking, "Why don't you just adopt?"

Unconditional Love in the Age of Conditional Reproduction

The increasing control that human beings can exercise over reproduction, from conception aids we buy at our local drugstore to IVF and genetic screening, is forcing us to examine more closely our motives and desires for having children. As theologian Bonnie J. Miller-McLemore explains, "In a way unprecedented in human history, as a result of new technologies and the population explosion, parents can no longer enter into parenthood blithely and unreflectively. People must now weigh carefully the validity and merits of their often preconscious and sometimes rather self-centered motives to reproduce themselves."

Some ethicists worry that the ability use both low- and high-tech reproductive tools to control our procreation—even when we are simply using contraception to avoid having children at certain times and ovulation-predictor kits to maximize our chances of conceiving when we want to—will erode one of the fundamental qualities of good parents: unconditional love. Ethicists worry that "parents will be led by science to forget that unconditional love is a signal requirement of being a parent."

In the next chapter I will look more closely at the pressures modern parents face, from within and without, to bear certain types of children—independent and healthy children, who will not be an undue burden on either their parents or society. The ability to control when and how we have children, as well as (to some extent) what kind of children we will have, certainly presents a temptation for parents to make their love conditional, rejecting any child who does not fit their and society's vision of the "perfect" child. However, we need to remember that even parents who conceive children in the old-fashioned way, without any technological assistance, have children for a variety of motives and have hopes and dreams for what their children will be like. It is a mistake to believe that conception via sexual intercourse always or more easily leads to unconditional parental love and acceptance. People who conceive easily can be terrible parents. They can abort babies with treatable ailments, such as cleft palates, or those who are not of the desired gender. They can insist that their bookish, artistic son play sports because Dad once dreamed of being a professional ballplayer. Likewise, parents who use IVF to conceive twins or triplets can be profoundly grateful for the children they bear, even if those children are not perfectly healthy.

One of the most maddening truths of this imperfect world, particularly vexing for those who struggle to conceive children whom they desperately want, is that many kinds of sexual intercourse between many sorts of people can lead to conception. The sex may be pleasurable or not, loving or indifferent, violent or gentle, carefully planned or spur-of-the-moment, between hormonal teenagers or spouses who have been together for years—and none of these factors influence whether the sex leads to a baby or not. It is unfair to characterize natural conception as the fruit of a loving union, and technological conception as a pragmatic tool for getting just the kind of baby we want.

Modern parents face tremendous pressures to be the right kind of parents to the right kind of children. Our goal in examining reproductive ethics should not be to classify all natural conception as open and loving, and all technological conception as conditional and controlling. Rather, let's explore how, given the available technology as well as societal expectations of all parents, we can model God's unconditional love for everyone in a world that celebrates achievement, perfection, and getting what we want when we want it.

Questions to Think About

1. What do you think are some of the most powerful motives for people to have children? If you have or plan to have children, what did or does motivate you?
2. How does a Christian view of parenthood as a vocation differ from cultural assumptions about whether and why people have children?
3. Do you see a difference between procreation and reproduction? How do you view Christian perspectives on the relationship among sex, procreation, and marriage?
4. What are your views or your experiences of adoption? Is it reasonable or ethical for people to pursue assisted reproduction rather than adopting a child?
5. What concerns, if any, does technological reproduction raise when it comes to parents' unconditional love of their children?

3

Without a Map

The Blessings and Burdens of Choice

*U*ntil we learned that my OI mutation had been found, Daniel and I kept our conversations about PGD between ourselves. I knew that, no matter what we decided, some people would believe we had made the wrong choice. Some would feel it was unethical to conceive a baby who could have a serious genetic disorder. I knew a woman with OI who had an unplanned pregnancy, and when she decided to have the baby, her sister stopped speaking to her because she was so scandalized that someone would choose to bear a child at high risk for such a significant disorder. (We were fortunate that, if we did have family members or friends who thought we took too big a risk in having Leah, they kept it to themselves.) Others would feel that it was unethical to manipulate the mechanics of human conception so that our baby could be free of OI. We realized that our decision was ultimately between us and God. But now that PGD was a real possibility, we carefully approached several people and invited them into our conversations.

We began by tackling the most concrete part of our dilemma: the money. Using PGD involves going through all the steps of a normal IVF cycle. I would give myself injections for several weeks to stimulate my ovaries. During those weeks, I would have numerous ultrasounds and blood tests to see whether the injections were working. Once ultrasounds revealed several mature eggs, I would be sedated while the eggs were being retrieved from my ovaries. The eggs would be fertilized by Daniel's sperm, then allowed to mature for several days until each consisted of six to eight cells. One cell from each fertilized egg would be taken out and sent to Chicago, where

a lab would test them to see which had my OI mutation. The fertilized eggs that did not have the OI mutation would be put back in my
uterus, and I would continue taking hormones by injection for two
weeks, until a pregnancy test told us whether the cycle had worked.

The IVF cycle alone—medications, blood tests, ultrasounds,
retrieval, and embryo transfer—would cost $8,000 to $10,000. On
top of that, we would pay about $5,000 to a Chicago lab to do genetic
testing. This money would cover a onetime fee for them to develop
a unique test for locating my mutation, as well as the actual testing.
The total cost would be about $15,000 for our first IVF cycle, and
about $12,000 for any subsequent cycles. (The cost of developing a
test for my specific OI mutation would be reflected only in the first
cycle's fees.)

Daniel's employer, a large university, offered an insurance rider
that covered 80 percent of IVF costs for three cycles—for people
who were infertile, which we were not. The chipper young woman
at the Center who shepherded patients through the financial side of
IVF promised that she would help us try to convince the university to
cover our cycles under the IVF rider, if we would agree to pay for the
genetic testing ourselves. Even if we secured the insurance coverage,
we had to come up with the other 20 percent of the regular IVF costs,
plus the genetic testing costs. We decided to ask Daniel's mom if
she would consider helping us out. When she eventually agreed, she
reported a brief conversation she had with her pastor. He had coun-
seled that, because we would not be creating embryos to be used for
scientific experiments, he did not see any ethical objections to my
mother-in-law's financial support.

Besides wondering how we would pay for PGD, I was consumed
with thinking about whether or not it was the right thing to do. Was
it right to manipulate life in this way to avoid a nonfatal disorder,
especially when I knew firsthand that affected people could live hap-
pily with it and in spite of it? Was it reasonable to spend money on
avoiding this one type of suffering when there are so many other,
more fundamental kinds of suffering in the world? I longed to wrestle with these questions in the company of someone who shared
our faith. My mother-in-law's pastor's response seemed simplistic
and superficial. Weren't there more questions at stake here, beyond
the use of embryos for scientific experiments? In the months to

come, though, I learned that this pastor's response was typical of Christians who considered the ethics of IVF or PGD. Few delved very deep, limiting their examination to fairly simple formulas of right and wrong. For example, if PGD helps limit suffering, it is a good thing. Or PGD is just another medical technology that people have developed with their God-given intellect; if coronary bypass and arthroscopic knee surgery are ethically sound, then so is PGD. Though I wanted to accept these conclusions—they all supported my desire for conceiving a healthy baby through PGD—I was unsettled. I needed to dig deeper.

There is a reservoir in our town, with several lakes surrounded by oaks and maples, and rocky outcrops pushing up from the soil like fists. On the path around the reservoir, Daniel and I have talked through all the major decisions of our married life. In the spring and summer of 2002, with the burden of our PGD decision weighing heavily, we talked about our choices. I often became angry during these talks, not at Daniel, but at having to hold these discussions at all, and at how unequipped we and everyone around us were for having anything useful to say. I felt like we were walking through a treacherous mountain path, yet without map or compass, unsure which way to go. Everyone we called on our cell phone for help listened kindly and then said something like, "Well, you could go right or you could go left. Just watch out for cougars, and don't twist your ankle in a hole."

On one reservoir walk, as we came upon a narrow bridge across the water, I spat out, "What if we try PGD and end up with a kid without OI, but who has some other problem? What if we end up saying, 'If we hadn't screwed with nature this way, this wouldn't have happened?'" I knew that PGD did not make our risk of other genetic anomalies greater. But I also felt that, by trying to take charge of a process that was historically out of human control, we would bear greater responsibility for whatever came of that process, for good or ill. Somehow, whatever happened would be partly our responsibility because we had chosen to make it so.

I dwelled less on the standard questions surrounding reproductive issues, such as the status of the embryo as a human being, than on my own shame and guilt that I was even considering PGD. My form of OI is not fatal. Though it causes significant disability, pain, and more (for example, I developed a bone infection at age six that made me seriously ill), it is still a milder form of the disorder than many people live with. I felt selfish for wanting to banish even this modest level of disability from my family. Every time I read a news article about starving and sick children in other parts of the world, I felt ashamed for wanting to spend tens of thousands of dollars just to ensure that my well-fed, loved, and privileged child would also have the benefit of good health. I also feared that I would be contributing to a society that would become less and less tolerant of disabilities as technology makes it easier to avoid them.

I also obsessed about the increased chance that we would have twins if we conceived through PGD, because conception via IVF is more likely than natural conception to result in a multiple pregnancy. My body handled my first pregnancy well, but I was pregnant with a single, fairly small baby. Two babies would probably mean bed rest and potentially dangerous stress on my fragile bones and joints. The higher risk of premature births in a multiple pregnancy meant that we might end up with strong-boned kids who also had cerebral palsy, cognitive disability, or some other problem associated with prematurity. Though I handled the physical labor of childcare rather well, my caring for even one child requires more stamina, creativity, and energy than it does for more physically able mothers. I cannot carry a child in one arm and a shopping bag or laundry basket in the other, for example, because I always need one hand free to keep my balance or hold a stair banister. Pushing a double stroller would be hard work for me; if I gave birth to twins, I would probably need a triple stroller because Leah was still not walking on her own. I imagined myself as a prisoner in my own home, unable to go anywhere with Leah and a pair of twins because of the sheer effort involved in getting all those nonwalking beings from point A to point B.

Daniel was less troubled by our decision than I was. I bore the brunt of our decision. My body would be manipulated, my bad gene would be weeded out, I would live with the physical consequences of a multiple pregnancy, and I would do most of the phone calling and paperwork to figure out how we would pay for PGD. Daniel said that if I decided I could not go forward with PGD, he would accept that. But his desire for a healthy child was strong, and he clung to everything we or someone else said to support PGD as a valid decision. Nonetheless, he shared some of my ambivalence and knew I was struggling to figure out the right thing to do, so he wrote a brief e-mail to some friends we had known in D.C., asking for prayers and advice.

We met Chris and Hannah Roberts in 1997, when both they and we were newlyweds. Though we moved from D.C. only fourteen months later, we formed a lasting friendship that continued after we settled in Connecticut and they moved to London, where Chris was studying for his PhD in Christian ethics. We confided in Chris and Hannah not because of Chris's field of study, but because we trusted them to be honest and thoughtful. Thus began a nine-month cyber conversation on our PGD dilemma. Chris and I did almost all of the e-mailing, copying the messages to our spouses; we were both writers who found our computer keyboards a comfortable place to hash out complex, difficult questions. Much later, when our dilemma was behind us, Chris suggested that I use our e-mail correspondence to write an article on our PGD experience. An article became a memoir, which eventually became this book.

In his initial e-mail response, Chris raised a number of issues— none of which were the ones I was so concerned with at the time. In this and the following chapters, I will occasionally refer to my e-mail exchange with Chris. That exchange not only offers some interesting perspectives but also models a nontraditional method of practical ethics. Rather than consulting scholarly texts written by theologians or ethicists, I corresponded with a friend, who was academically gifted and extremely knowledgeable, but who always addressed my particular situation, taking my story and my gut feelings into account. For example, Chris once brought up some media accounts related to assisted reproduction, remarking that the cultural attitudes expressed by people interviewed for the stories worried him because they were so focused on personal fulfillment, choice, and control. But, he went on, "you have helped me imagine a different way of seeing reproductive technology—of seeing that it is not always 'in general in our culture' and can be seen as 'in this instance for Daniel and Ellen.'" I have come to believe that hearing, accepting, and responding directly to people's unique stories is vital for meaningful ethical discussions.

Chris quickly dispatched our worries about money. He was not concerned with the financial resources we might spend "on creating this kid with strong bones when there's so much suffering in the world . . . in the sense that I'm not bothered by the money involved being spent on your personal issues. . . . This is your suffering and it is very real to you, and it is your vocation to struggle with the suffering of OI in a way in which it is not your vocation to struggle with famine or war (for example)." Throughout our correspondence, Chris urged us to look beyond the practical questions that occupied us, to see instead the larger truths of what our faith says about human life in relationship with God. For example, he raised the question of whether it is our duty as parents, and particularly as Christian parents, to minimize our children's suffering:

> I think it is vital that you understand that minimizing your children's suffering is not the same as good parenting. . . . To say it another way: As much as you love your actual or potential children and want them to flourish, your first duty as a parent is to model a life for your children which is based on the love of God and the joyful fruit of your faith. Your first duty as a parent is to be faithful in your attempt to follow Christ. And we know where a life of discipleship ultimately leads, . . . to the cross, which our culture/friends/family often have a hard time understanding. This way means treating life as a gift that is not ours to do with what we will, and it is opposed to doing everything conceivable to clear the possible pain of life out of the way of your kids. . . . Our culture, and hence most of the doctors and parents and friends and advisors you are likely to meet in this situation, tend to work from a different premise. Their highest value is that if you have the opportunity to minimize suffering, it's a sin against compassion not to take the opportunity. From a Christian point of view, that can't be sufficient. . . .
>
> Christians are trying to trust and follow a God who assumed flesh, got wounded and brutalized, became weak and dependent in order to love and show us a model of human life. The conclusion Christian theology has traditionally drawn is not that suffering and weakness are good in themselves (they're not), but that . . . suffering and weakness are not the ultimate disasters. In God's eyes, which are the only eyes that matter ultimately, a flourishing human being is not the same thing as a human being free from suffering.

And that is something . . . we must testify to our children, over against our culture, which preaches happiness only in things like strength, sexiness, romance, adventure, perfection, etc. Which is just a recipe for fear (that we'll lose those very precarious goods) or envy (that others have them and we don't).

Again and again I have returned to this idea that avoidance of suffering, even for our children, is not our highest moral duty. This truth is both obvious and elusive. Parents accept the inevitability of our children's suffering all the time. We hold their hands as they scream through painful medical procedures we consented to on their behalf. We make our son apologize to the grouchy neighbor whose window he broke. We refuse to beg the teacher to change a failing grade even when it means our daughter won't graduate with her friends. We explain that "life isn't fair" because we know from experience that it surely isn't.

At times we even cause our children's suffering. We yell when we should soothe. We answer a phone call when a child is midstory. In anger we assault our children with words like "selfish" and "careless," with slammed doors and pounding fists on tables. We cannot protect our children from all suffering, and we will inevitably cause them to suffer—that is a central, heartbreaking truth of parenting.

But parents also find and seize plenty of opportunities to help our children avoid suffering. We take them to the doctor, feed them healthy food, and institute rules about where they can go, what they can do, and with whom. When we see our kids making choices that we know will lead them to suffer, such as neglecting schoolwork, drinking too much, or dating an abusive partner, we offer every resource we can to support them in making better choices. When we're dealing with a specific kind of suffering—that caused by a particular disorder or illness, with inevitable painful effects—it is terribly hard to reject the opportunity to help our kids avoid suffering, especially when we have firsthand knowledge of exactly what kind of suffering we're talking about. I responded to Chris by saying:

> [Sometimes I feel] that going the [PGD] route would be an attempt to take control, in essence to take control away from God and put it in our (and our doctors') hands. That we would be saying, . . . "Okay, God, you've blessed us with this beautiful daughter, and

you've protected her from a lot of pain and suffering thus far, and we are more fortunate than we deserve to be. . . . But next time, we're not going to trust you so much. We're going to do what we can so we never have to feel the way we felt the day Leah was diagnosed. Yes, you brought us out of that dark place, but we don't want to have to ask you to do that again." That feels unfaithful to me. On the other hand, I do really start to lose it when I think about going through that diagnosis again. The day we got Leah's diagnosis was the worst day of my life. . . . I don't want to go through the pain of watching my next child being left behind by his/her peers. . . . I don't want to spend my child's second birthday in the emergency room (as we did on Leah's second birthday). A lot of our fear . . . is less about what our child will suffer . . . and more about what *we* will suffer in letting go of the dream of having a healthy child. . . . I know avoiding suffering is not what God calls us to, but it sure does sound nice.

I've come across people who observe, with an air of accusation, that parents who use PGD are as concerned with their own suffering as they are with their potential children's suffering. There should be no shame in admitting that. Such concern simply means that, like most human beings, we are daunted by the prospect of pain.

During our e-mail correspondence with Chris, Daniel and I also met with the rector of our Episcopal church. He declined to make a clear judgment about whether PGD was ethical for us, but he did caution us to avoid the pitfall of thinking that something is morally wrong just because it is not "natural." Medical technology allows us to overcome many "natural" diseases and injuries that killed people in generations past. Like my mother-in-law's pastor's advice, this seemed reasonable enough but did not address the more subtle discomfort I had about PGD. Unlike other medical technologies, PGD alters the way we receive God's most fundamental gift: life. Medical treatments alleviate suffering by caring for people who already exist. Successful PGD cycles alleviate suffering by ensuring that people affected by particular medical problems do not exist, because they are never born.

Our pastor also felt that if we decided to conceive on our own, we had to do so with our hearts open to whatever happened. He cautioned that perceiving natural conception as a gamble, with one outcome representing a win (no OI) and the other representing a loss (OI), was dangerous. We had to willingly and eagerly accept the gift of life in whatever form it came to us. That rang true; all parents should consider their ability to accept a less than perfectly healthy child before conceiving (though many parents don't). But it seemed a tall order. I knew I would grieve a second child's OI diagnosis as much as I had Leah's.

We left that meeting still uncertain. But we felt a little more clear that we, as Christian people, could see PGD as an ethically viable choice, although one made with the fear and trembling that accompany all great life choices. I also knew in my gut that I could not conceive a baby naturally without wishing and hoping for that child to be free of OI.

In the end, we both just grew tired of thinking about PGD so much. We wanted a baby. We wanted a healthy baby. And PGD was a possibility for us, so we decided to try it. After we made our decision, I wrote again to Chris to explain:

> I imagined how I would feel if we had another child diagnosed with OI (devastated) vs. how it would feel to be pregnant knowing there was only the slimmest chance our child would have OI or any other disorder. The word that came to mind was "freedom." I sat with that realization for a few days, trying to determine if I was falsely thinking that PGD would offer freedom from suffering. But I realized how deeply I desired freedom from OI—at least in this one decision.

Around the time we decided to try PGD, Leah finally began walking independently, at nearly two and a half years old. We reveled in seeing her upright after many months of her scooting around on her bottom. But her new mobility brought new risks. There was a several-week period when she fell many times, and each time clutched at her right ankle, near where she had fractured it on her second birthday. She begged me through her tears, "Mommy, make it better! Kiss it better!" Despite her progress, the pain of life with OI still regularly broke our hearts. As I wrote to Chris, "I know that such heartache is just part of parenting any child, healthy or not. It's just that this particular brand of heartache has worn out its welcome in my life."

Parents under Pressure

Parents in twenty-first-century America are under a lot of pressure to do the right thing by their children. Although most people recognize that parents cannot fully protect their children from pain, injury, and illness, parents are regularly bombarded with messages that they should strive to do just that. To get a sense of the pressures that reasonable, thoughtful American parents face daily, here are a few anecdotes from my own suburban life showing how ready people are to judge parents as careless:

- A friend left her four children, ages three to ten, in her minivan as she went into a gas station's convenience store. The cashier wondered aloud if it was safe for her to leave her kids in the car. My friend had decided that it was better to leave them in the car, which was parked within sight of the cash register, rather than parade four children across a busy parking lot. But she was so shaken by the cashier's accusatory tone that when the phone rang later that day and her caller ID said the call came from the social services department, she was sure the cashier had called to report her for negligence. The phone call was actually from a friend and was unrelated to the incident.
- During a heat wave when Leah was about seven months old, I decided that we needed to get out of our stuffy, non-air-conditioned apartment. I nursed her so she would be well-hydrated, slathered her in baby-safe sunscreen, and put her in a stroller, covered by a sunshade, with just a light T-shirt and diaper on. As I walked through the center of town, a woman I didn't know opened her car window and yelled to me, "You shouldn't have that baby out here in this heat!"
- One school year a father who regularly dropped off his daughter at the curb in front of our elementary school in the morning, allowing her to walk along the sidewalk to the fenced, teacher-supervised kindergarten playground by herself, was the subject of whispered conversations among other parents about his irresponsibility.

Most modern parents (particularly mothers, who have or are perceived as having primary responsibility for children's safety and well-being) can tell stories like these about others' judgment of their parenting choices. Parents are scolded for bottle-feeding in public, for breast-feeding in public, for letting the baby cry it out, for not letting the baby cry it out, for sleeping with the baby, for putting the baby in a crib, for not providing enough outdoor playtime, for letting the kids play outdoors without constant adult supervision. When it comes to parents' reproductive choices—how many children to have, when to have them, and what precautions and tests to take to ensure their health—the stakes are higher and the pressures greater.

A New Eugenics?

The term "eugenics," coined in the late nineteenth century, refers to selective breeding, in which people with desirable traits are encouraged to bear children (positive eugenics), and those with undesirable traits are discouraged or prevented from having children (negative eugenics). In the first half of the twentieth century, eugenic ideas took hold not only in Nazi Germany but also in the United States and other Western nations, which engaged in eugenic policies such as forced sterilization of people with mental illness and disabilities, and restrictions on the number of immigrants from cultural groups or nationalities perceived as intrinsically inferior. Although eugenics proponents often portrayed their beliefs as based on rational scientific principles, eugenic ideas were actually pseudoscientific. Programs to achieve racial purity, for example, relied on unproven assertions about the inherent qualities of racial and ethnic groups, while anti-immigrant policies rested in part on the belief that lower-class people were fundamentally less capable of learning and success than upper-class people.

Today some argue that PGD and prenatal diagnosis (with its underlying assumption that parents can terminate a pregnancy if the diagnosis is troubling) are modern embodiments of old eugenic ideas. Are they? Certainly these technologies, in part, try to predict a child's potential for success, independence, and health based on inherent qualities. They do rely on actual rather than pseudoscience; a baby with a gene that causes OI will have OI, a baby with three copies of chromosome 21 will have Down syndrome, and a baby who inherits two recessive cystic fibrosis genes will have cystic fibrosis. Those scientific facts are beyond dispute.

But even if modern reproductive technologies, unlike early twentieth-century eugenics, rely on scientific fact, they perpetuate the dangerous assumption that human lives can be judged based on a single inherent quality (in the old eugenics, one's race, ethnicity, or class; in the new eugenics, one's genetic identity). No one can predict exactly what even well-understood genetic facts will mean in the long term, in the context of a multifaceted human life. Yes, children possessing certain genes will have OI, Down syndrome, cystic fibrosis, or some other disorder. But we cannot know ahead of time whether those children will be happy or troubled, excel in some areas even if they struggle in others, or be the sources and the recipients of great love, acceptance, and joy. We cannot predict those things about any new baby, no matter the genetic makeup.

The ability to match certain problems to certain genes tempts us to forget that all human lives are subject to risks, known and unknown. My family history and Daniel's are great examples. My OI mutation was easy to target because it was known, it had predictable effects, and the physical ramifications of passing the mutation on were clear: Our child would break lots of bones. Daniel, coming from a family with a significant history of substance abuse and depression, as well as diabetes, brought plenty of genetic risk to our childbearing, but we didn't focus on those risks because, compared with OI, they are less understood, less precise, and less likely to affect our children when they are young. When we consider all the risks we subject our children to simply by having them—both obvious risks related to family history and the risks of living in a world where accident, illness, or various catastrophes can occur without warning—deciding which human lives are preferable based on one isolated trait begins to look a little ridiculous. Liza Mundy, who interviewed dozens of parents and prospective parents for her book on reproductive medicine, observed that a focus on reproductive liberty and "a trend toward compulsive micromanagement of every aspect of our children's lives . . . sometimes persuade would-be parents that they are entitled to pursue any avenue of reproductive technology, and to determine every aspect of the outcome. . . . And the ironic thing is—for me, this was a key revelation—determining the outcome is exactly what cannot be done."

There is one interesting factor to consider, though, before labeling genetic screening as a new eugenics. One might expect that Jewish people, having been the target not only of Nazi genocide but also of centuries' worth of discrimination and violence based on pseudoscientific notions of racial purity, would be particularly suspicious of any attempt to judge human worth based on genetic traits. Yet while Jewish authorities have ethical concerns with some aspects of assisted reproduction, the Jewish community has largely embraced genetic screening to lower the incidence of disorders that disproportionately affect Jews, such as Tay-Sachs disease. For example, the Brooklyn-based organization Dor Yeshorim maintains a registry of young unmarried Jews who voluntarily submit to genetic testing, to determine their carrier status for Tay-Sachs and several other recessive disorders. If a man and woman see potential for marriage, they can call Dor Yeshorim, type in a PIN, and learn whether both members of the couple are carriers for the same disorder. (With recessive disorders, carriers have the genetic mutation in question but are unaffected. If two carriers have a child, there is a 25 percent chance the child will inherit both parents' carrier genes and will therefore have the disorder, and a 50 percent chance the child will inherit one parent's gene and will therefore be an unaffected carrier.) If both would-be spouses are carriers for a disorder, it is recommended that they end their relationship. Dor Yeshorim is credited with lowering the incidence of several genetic disorders because most young people who use the service heed that recommendation. Also, because Jewish law does not consider a fertilized egg to have full human status until it is implanted in a mother's womb, PGD is generally acceptable for Jewish couples who wish to avoid passing on a recessive disorder. The Jewish experience illustrates that using genetic screening to ensure that children do not have devastating disorders cannot automatically be equated with eugenics. While I see the potential peril in judging whether human lives are worth living based on certain genetic traits, I also understand parental desires to bear children who are not at risk of inheriting specific disorders present in their family history.

"Justification by Meticulously Planned Procreation"

Our American culture values independence, choice, control, health, and success. We expect parents to exhibit those qualities and to carefully manage their reproduction and child rearing so that their offspring embody them as well. Parents perceived as careless are judged harshly. A concern with lax parenting led the cashier to question my friend's leaving her kids in the car, a stranger to question my taking the baby out on a hot day, and other parents to question a father's decision to let his daughter walk a few hundred feet by herself. That same concern, writ large, underlies cultural pressures for parents to make wise, risk-averse reproductive decisions about how many children to have, when to have them, and how to ensure their health and safety so they will grow into productive members of society, rather than being burdens on their families and communities. Values such as independence, health, and wealth stand in contrast to those of Christ and the early church, where the most dependent members of society (children, women, the sick, and the poor) were given places of honor; yet even American churches have endorsed these health-and-wealth values in advocating for responsible reproduction. And the backlash against parents perceived as careless is not only a twenty-first-century phenomenon.

Theologian Amy Laura Hall's fascinating book *Conceiving Parenthood: American Protestantism and the Spirit of Reproduction* examines how churches and middle-class culture have fostered a bias toward healthy, productive, independent, and proficient children who will not be a burden on society. Hall believes there is a "new eugenics" that relies on voluntary participation rather than coercion. By educating people about heredity with tools such as genetic counseling, the new eugenics, which emerged in the twentieth century, encourages parents to make choices to better their families and society. Unlike the old eugenics' focus on race and class, "the new science would take off race and class blinders to assess *all lineages* for their promise or peril." Hall argues that for much of the twentieth century, this focus on making responsible choices and having genetically advantaged children was reinforced by churches, which honored small, carefully planned, healthy, and well-groomed families as the ideal, and by the media, which advertised a variety of products to help parents raise their children in well-controlled, hygienic households.

Hall quotes from a 1926 sermon by Unitarian pastor Phillips Endicott Osgood: "Until sin and weakness and disease and pain are done away, we are only starting to commence to get ready to enter into life as it may be. . . . God the Refiner we know; do we yet dream of the skill or the beauty of purpose of God the Craftsman with his once purified silver? May the time soon come when in refined humanity he can see his own face, clear and unsullied." Osgood, according to Hall, "suggested that the culmination of God's creation was dependent on the elimination of suffering. This involved not acts of mercy toward the sick and the poor but acts to secure a future free of those who would 'handicap [the Spirit's] incarnation.'" In other words, eliminate suffering by preventing the births of those who suffer—the poor, the sick, the disabled.

In addition to frequently quoting church sources, Hall's book includes a number of fascinating early and mid-twentieth-century advertisements for products promoting clean, well-managed households, including Lysol, which was advertised not only as a tool for keeping germs away from children but also as a "feminine hygiene" product that would help women stay attractive and healthy by preventing pregnancies through Lysol douching. Hall argues persuasively that twentieth-century middle-class parents were subjected to powerful messages telling them that good parents shun carelessness in favor of scientifically informed and carefully managed reproduction and child rearing. This involved not only keeping children and households clean and healthy but also timing and, when necessary, preventing pregnancies, to keep families small and manageable. While some eugenic policies encouraged the most desirable types of people to have many children (such as Nazi Germany's *Lebensborn* program, which provided free health care and other incentives for Aryan women to bear children), the new eugenics assumed that prudent parents would limit their childbearing to ensure orderly households and adequate resources for children to grow into productive adults. According to Hall, middle-class, mainstream American Protestantism came to "epitomize *justification by meticulously planned procreation.*"

In a modern example of this phenomenon, Episcopal Presiding Bishop Katharine Jefferts Schori observed with pride, in a 2006 interview with the *New York Times Magazine*, that Episcopalians "tend to be better-educated and to reproduce at lower rates," compared with Roman Catholics and Mormons. Schori attributed Episcopalians' procreative restraint to environmental concern: "We encourage people to pay attention to the stewardship of the earth and not use more than their portion." Although she focused on environmental care rather than familial health or the need to raise self-sufficient children, her comments revealed that a Protestant emphasis on improving society through carefully controlled reproduction is alive and well here in the twenty-first century. In this model of thinking, children are reduced to great suckers-up of resources; prudent, educated people plan their procreation to minimize the damaging effects of their children's births.

Though Hall's book focuses on parenting ideals that emerged in the early and mid-twentieth century, she argues that the pressure on parents to exercise painstaking care over their reproductive decisions and their children persists. In interviewing women for her book, Hall writes:

> Women have explained (at times in excruciatingly painful detail) the pressure they feel under to conceive of parenthood in ways that involve meticulous timing and intense quality control. A woman described the pressure to time her pregnancies *just so* for the sake of optimal sibling relationships and college financing. A colleague described the importance of conceiving on time to maximize limited maternity leave, and to schedule a medically non-necessary cesarean to minimize interruption from work. Another beloved friend described the pressure that led her to terminate one twin with Down syndrome for the sake of the other, "normal" twin sharing her womb. Another told of the pressure she felt to achieve what has come to be called "gender balancing" through selective in vitro fertilization. Many mothers related the pressure they felt to watch for even a week's delay in the *to-be-expected* timing for the first recognizable smile, bowel movement, full night's sleep, for weight gain (for baby) and weight loss (for mother); the pressure to find the optimal preschool, elementary teacher, and gifted program; the pressure, in sum, to give birth to and then form a child who will cohere to the expectations of her family, friends, and neighbors.

Hall also heard stories from parents who "have children deemed as those-to-be avoided. . . . These are children who, by the same logic of choosiness pressuring many white, upper-middle-class pregnancies, seem inadequately *planned*, whether due to disability, spacing, maternal age, race, or some combination of these."

Churches and the media have not been the only voices telling parents it is their duty to make scientifically informed, deliberate childbearing decisions for the good of their families and the wider society. Recall the interview with Nobel prizewinner Robert Edwards, the British fertility medicine pioneer who participated in the first IVF procedure to result in a live birth in 1978. As I discussed in the introduction, Edwards boldly said, "Soon it will be a sin of parents to have a child that carries the heavy burden of genetic disease. We are entering a world where we have to consider the quality of our children."

The moral danger of using the term "quality" in reference to children should be apparent, particularly to those who profess belief in a loving God. Children are not products to be manufactured to parental specifications and subjected to parental or cultural approval: they are gifts to be loved and accepted as they are.

Further, determining who is and who is not worthy of life, even when we do so using objective scientific criteria such as the presence or absence of certain genetic traits, requires subjective evaluation of those traits. Which genetic disorders can be reasonably accommodated, and which cause suffering significant enough to justify weeding them out? Who defines "significant enough"? Do we look only at the potential for genetic mutations to shorten life span or cause significant physical distress, or might some parents also consider the social ramifications of certain genes—their potential to limit academic and employment success or foster social exclusion? If a parent argues that her frizzy hair or nearsightedness has caused real suffering (due to relentless teasing from peers, for example), might she argue that it is reasonable to use PGD to ensure that those traits are not passed on? And what are the consequences of changing cultural expectations and scientific progress? As genetic science learns more about what is written into our cells, it is likely that everyone—even those who appear strong and healthy—will have their genetic flaws revealed and may become subjected to ever-higher standards for acceptable levels of risk, difference, disability, and disease.

As a Christian and a self-professed laid-back mother, I am troubled by the idea that parents can supposedly control their children's ultimate health, happiness, and success by making responsible choices about pregnancy timing, family size, income, diet, discipline, education, and a host of other child-rearing decisions. While the "quality control" ethic is frequently cited in theological discussions about reproductive and genetic technology, I agree with Hall that all modern American parents, not just those who explore or use reproductive technology, are expected to carefully plan, control, and nurture their children to ensure that they will grow up as productive members of society. And troublesome children are often blamed on careless parents. At one time or another in parenting debates (breast vs. bottle, public school vs. home school, "free-range" parents vs. "helicopter" parents, and so forth), each side accuses the other of ruining the children—their physical health, their mental well-being, and/or their ability to succeed in school, relationships, and the "real world."

Christians in particular, believing that all people are made in God's image, have a duty to remind prospective parents that, as theologian John Swinton puts it, "We are not commodities to be bought and sold. We are first and foremost persons, loved and valued just as we are because that is what God is and what God does." In addition our culture puts great value on individuals' right to make choices and also on individuals' responsibility to bear the consequences of those choices. It is not hard to imagine that in the future, when reproductive and genetic technology will potentially be available to everyone, parents could be subjected to concrete consequences if they choose *not* to exercise "quality control" over their children. Given how easily our culture already vilifies parents who are perceived as irresponsible, it seems quite possible that we will decide that communities have no obligation to support children with disabilities (through government-funded health insurance, early intervention services, special education services, or accessibility requirements) because their parents could have chosen not to bear those children.

The Tension between Private Decisions
and Public Consequences

Although I am concerned about the cultural consequences of per-ceiving children as commodities over whom we exercise control, I am also convinced that most prospective parents who use reproduc-tive technology do not see their children that way. Rather, they are motivated by understandable desires to raise happy, healthy children without more than their fair share of heartbreak. That was certainly my and Daniel's motivation in pursuing PGD to conceive a second child. It would have been impossible for us to look at our beloved Leah and talk about "quality control" or a desire to get a better prod-uct next time around, as if we were talking about a disappointing restaurant meal or a new car that had failed to live up to its advertised hype. Likewise, though I have read plenty of scholarly bioethics dis-cussions in researching this book, the most valuable resources have been other families' stories. I am convinced by reading and hearing others' stories that most of those who use reproductive technology are motivated simply by the love of parents for their children. Peo-ple do not make decisions about their cherished babies in the public square, where we need to rightly be concerned about questions such as the commodification of children and the value of people with dis-abilities. Parents make these decisions with their hearts as well as their minds. Though the cultural questions of where reproductive technology is leading us are vital, it is not fair to lay the weight of those questions on the shoulders of individual parents who are just trying to do their very best for their potential or actual children.

Although new technologies raise ethical questions that demand our attention, we need to keep in mind two important observations. First, as author Randi Hutter Epstein illustrates in her 2010 book on the history of childbirth, which details historical efforts by both women and medical providers to control the outcome of a fundamen-tally unpredictable process, "the quest for the perfect offspring was a goal since antiquity, not simply a notion prompted by modern medi-cine." For much of human history, pregnancy and childbirth were entirely overseen by women who offered folk wisdom to ensure safe births and healthy babies. When male physicians became involved, they brought an air of scientific authority and tools perceived as so necessary for ensuring the health of mother and baby that one family of doctors kept their forceps design a tightly guarded secret for decades. The rise of hospital births came out of the same emphasis on hygienic practices to produce healthy families that Amy Laura Hall identified in her book on middle-class reproduction. The desire to minimize the great risks and unknown consequences of conceiving and bearing brand-new people is not new.

Second, those who conceive children with the help of medical technology are often more, not less, aware of their children as gifts. As Liza Mundy observes after interviewing many couples who used reproductive technology, "The truth is that many fertility patients are deeply grateful for what they get, and what they get sometimes are children who are at a disadvantage [because of the increased risk of multiple births and associated problems], not unfairly enhanced."

Judgment Starts at Home

Recent legal and policy developments have somewhat eased my fears that our society will eventually require parents to use reproductive technology to ensure that their children don't have significant genetic conditions. For example, the 2009 Genetic Information Nondiscrimination Act prohibits employers from requesting genetic information or using that information in hiring, firing, and promoting decisions. It also prevents employers or health insurers from requiring employees to give their family medical histories. The 2010 Affordable Health Care for America Act (the Obama administration's health-care reform legislation) prohibits insurance companies from denying coverage based on preexisting conditions and allows children to be covered under their parents' insurance until age twenty-six.

But legal and policy solutions only do so much. Daily interactions with family members, friends, neighbors, and strangers send powerful messages about our cultural assumptions concerning parental responsibility for children's well-being. The anecdotes I mentioned earlier in this chapter illustrate the pressures that parents face, regardless of legal or medical fact or policy. On that hot summer day, I'm certain that if I had asked Leah's pediatrician whether it was safe to take a well-nourished, sunscreen-protected infant out for a stroll in ninety-five-degree heat, he would have said, "Of course." It was neither illegal nor against school policy for that dad to drop his kindergartener off at the sidewalk instead of walking her to the playground gate. But in both cases, other people's perceptions of risk and parental carelessness proved to be more powerful than facts about what is actually safe or legal.

In talking with other families living with genetic disabilities, I have been struck by how often the parents are subjected to judgment and pressure, sometimes from strangers, but also from friends, medical providers, and family members. Consider these parents who have told me their stories:*

Alyssa has Marfan syndrome, a connective tissue disorder that, like OI, has a 50 percent inheritance rate. Alyssa has chronic pain and some limitations on her physical activity, but for the most part, she lives a full, active life with the support of a loving family. She and her husband considered using PGD to ensure their first child would not inherit the disorder, but they chose not to. Her family supported her decision, and she gave birth to a daughter who did not inherit Marfan. But when she announced two years later that she was expecting a second child, a beloved uncle shocked her by saying he questioned Alyssa's judgment for choosing to take the risk a second time. To Alyssa, it felt like her uncle was questioning *her* worth by saying that having a baby who might inherit her disorder shows poor judgment.

Lucy's first child was born with significant physical and intellectual disabilities as a result of a genetic anomaly. When Lucy became pregnant with her second child, she was still in her early 30s, and her first child's condition was an isolated event, not due to a family history. In other words, she did not face any greater risk of genetic anomalies in her second pregnancy than any other healthy woman in her early 30s. Nevertheless, many people assumed she should, and would, get extensive prenatal testing this time around to ensure that she wouldn't have two disabled children. "The fact that we were being offered the testing seemed to imply [that] it was the medically appropriate or responsible thing

---

*Names and some identifying details of Alyssa's and Lucy's stories have been changed to protect their privacy.

to do," recalls Lucy. "An unfortunate corollary of that, which soon entered my mind, was that if we didn't have the testing, people would think we had chosen to have a child with a disability—or that we had somehow caused it or failed to prevent it (even though prevention in this case meant eliminating the child)." Lucy felt particularly pressured by medical personnel. When she saw a doctor to discuss amniocentesis, the doctor initially dismissed her as too young to undergo the process. But once he discovered that her first child was significantly disabled, the doctor's tone changed. He now understood "why you would want to do everything in your power to avoid having another abnormal baby." Lucy ended up getting an amniocentesis despite serious misgivings. "Everything inside of me was screaming, 'No, no, no—don't touch my baby,'" Lucy remembers. "But my fear of the judgment of others, should I not test and give birth to a child with disabilities, was greater. I was young and lacked the confidence to do what I felt was right, regardless of what others thought."

The Blessing and Burden of Reproductive Choice

By offering unprecedented knowledge of and control over conception, pregnancy, and birth, reproductive technology has in some ways been a blessing for parents and their children. For example, the extensive prenatal tests that have become routine in pregnancy led to a friend's being diagnosed with idiopathic thrombocytopenic purpura (ITP)—essentially, low blood platelet counts—during her second pregnancy. That knowledge allowed her doctors to manage her pregnancy and birth safely (no epidural, for example, because of increased bleeding risk) and also led my friend to decide against having any more children, because the risks associated with ITP, for both mother and baby, go up with each subsequent pregnancy.

Prenatal diagnosis of fetal abnormalities allows parents and medical personnel to prepare for the birth of a sick child, not only medically but also emotionally. Some people feel that parents' desire to know whether their child has medical problems before birth is a sign of our culture's addiction to control and our unwillingness to receive children just as they are. I will discuss this more in a later chapter, but in general I think that knowing ahead of time that a baby has health problems can be very helpful for parents. Dayna Olson-Getty has written about discovering, during her first pregnancy, that her baby had significant anomalies and would not survive long after birth. That knowledge allowed her and her husband time to grieve the diagnosis and prepare to welcome their son nonetheless. They planned how they wanted to spend the short time they had with their son after his birth; for example, they were prepared to tell the nurses who kept coming to take the baby away after he died that they wanted more time. They arranged for a photographer to chronicle the few hours they spent with their baby. If their son's condition had been a complete surprise, they would not have grieved either more or less than they did, but they would have had to make many decisions on the spot, in the midst of absorbing unexpected, tragic news.

But the choices made possible by technology bring significant burdens as well. The pressures imposed by cultural values, other people's assumptions, and the technology itself not only make some choices harder but also constrain parents' choices in some circumstances. It is difficult, for example, to forgo prenatal testing or continue carrying a baby that has been diagnosed with a serious problem if your family members and medical providers make clear that responsible parents don't give birth to sick babies. In a culture that values choice and control, the problem is not only that parents *want* choice and control over their childbearing decisions but also that everyone else *expects* parents to exercise choice and control.

The flip side of choice is responsibility. Our culture values individuals' freedom of choice, so long as they take responsibility for those choices. Parental responsibility for children's well-being can be a great burden, as I sensed when I wondered aloud how we would feel if our child, conceived through PGD to be free of OI, ended up with some other problem. As Christian bioethicist Gilbert Meilaender put it, "If we create a product for certain purposes, we can be held responsible for the quality of that product. As the technology makes possible a more complete responsibility for the child's well-being, so it also lays upon all who use it a heavier burden of responsibility. Complete freedom, godlike freedom, gives rise to utter responsibility."

Some years ago the *New York Times Magazine* ran an article by editor Bill Keller that illustrates well the terrible responsibility that comes with increased reproductive choice enabled by technology. Keller and his wife decided to terminate a pregnancy with a baby prenatally diagnosed with devastating abnormalities. Keller comments, "No one mandates prenatal testing, although it is such an automatic part of the regimen that many expectant mothers believe it is obligatory, and few fight it. My wife is a testing skeptic. She is convinced that if we had just let nature take its course, without sonograms and amniocentesis, 'we would have lost that baby, but we would not have killed that baby.'"

Technology such as prenatal testing, presented as offering greater choice, becomes socially enforced so that certain choices are expected and applauded while others are discouraged. As Meilaender has observed, "The technology carries its own momentum which, if not irresistible, is nevertheless very powerful."

Reproductive and genetic technologies are hard to resist in a culture emphasizing that parents are expected to make their children's well-being, health, and success their top priority in every decision, and to shield children from risk whenever possible, whether the risk involves genetic disease or sunburn. When prospective parents end up at the fertility clinic to learn more about technologies such as IVF and PGD, they become immersed in a medical culture whose values often mirror those of the wider culture, with a focus on choice, control, and success. In the next chapter, I'll look more closely at how medical and consumer cultures intersect at the fertility clinic, making informed, thoughtful, and ethical choices even more difficult for patients.

Questions to Think About

1. Do parents have an obligation to minimize their children's suffering?
2. What are some prevalent cultural expectations for American parents today, and what cultural values do those expectations reflect? How do those values compare with Christian values?
3. Do reproductive technologies such as IVF and PGD make children into products subject to "quality control"? Or is it reasonable for parents to use these technologies out of concern for their children's health and well-being?
4. Is the increasing choice and control that parents have over reproduction more a blessing or a burden?

4

The Slippery Slope

When Money and Medicine Meet at the Fertility Clinic

As the summer of 2002 wore on, Daniel and I were immersed in the convoluted and slow process of getting started with IVF. In June we attended a class at the Center for Advanced Reproductive Services at the University of Connecticut, where one of the physicians explained the IVF process in detail—the medications, ultrasounds, blood tests, retrieval, embryo transfer, and bed rest. Anyone going through IVF was required to complete the class before the Center would begin an IVF cycle. More than halfway through the class, a woman blew into the room and noisily took a seat. When the class ended, she rushed up to the doctor, complaining loudly that the directions she had been given to the classroom were confusing, which was why she missed most of the class. She demanded to know what missing the class would mean for her because she was planning on beginning her cycle the following week and would not accept a delay. The doctor—the same young, awkward doctor we had met with—blinked a few times and assured her he would look at her file. I never saw this woman again, but that brief exchange, similar in tone to those that take place at airline ticket counters when a flight has just been canceled, illustrates some of the perils of transforming reproduction into a fee-for-service business.

As the months went on and we wore ourselves out discussing the IVF process, I became increasingly disenchanted with the Center. Staff members were technically proficient, cheerful, and kind, but they seemed to be ill-equipped for—even uninterested in—addressing the nonmedical dilemmas we faced. This became most apparent as we struggled with how to pay for our first cycle of PGD. Although

Daniel's mother had agreed to give us some money toward the procedure and we were cautiously moving ahead, we still needed to know if Daniel's employer's IVF insurance rider would partially cover our expenses even though we were not infertile. If his employer did not agree to cover us under the rider, PGD was financially impossible. The young assistant at the Center who had earlier pledged to use her savvy and experience with insurance companies to help convince Daniel's employer to cover us now claimed she was unable to help. She seemed confused when I asked if she would call his employer on our behalf to explain that our procedure would differ from regular IVF only in the added step of genetic testing, which we would pay for on our own. She said that, because his employer was not an insurance company with whom the Center had an established contractual relationship, she could not become involved. I ended up calling Daniel's employer to explain our situation on my own.

Only later did I figure out that our request—that the Center help us pull together our finances *before* we committed to starting our PGD cycle—was unusual. The Center was apparently used to dealing with people who would do anything, including maxing out credit cards or taking out second mortgages, to conceive a baby. When I explained that figuring out how to *pay for* PGD was one factor in our decision whether to *try* PGD, the financial counselor looked at me like I was speaking a foreign language. Nevertheless, she finally provided me with a list of the procedures we would undergo as part of PGD, which I faxed to Daniel's employer to show that all of them except the genetic testing were standard IVF procedures. The employer agreed to reimburse 80 percent of our IVF costs. Between the insurance coverage and the help from Daniel's mom, the way was now clear to try one cycle of PGD.

We attended another class at the Center in August, this time to learn how to give injections of fertility hormones that would cause my ovaries to produce mature eggs for retrieval. We practiced snapping the top off glass vials of powder, mixing the powder with sterile water, and jabbing needles into oranges. The Center gave us a personalized binder with our instructions for the cycle. I was to begin giving myself ovary-stimulating medications via subcutaneous injection (into the skin of my abdomen or thigh) on Monday, September 2, 2002—Labor Day.

As we prepared for our first IVF/PGD cycle, the reality of having a child with OI hit us hard. In May, Leah had begun walking. In mid-June, I noticed a strange bump on the outside of her left forearm. An X-ray revealed a healing fracture, about ten days old. We were stunned. Leah had not acted like she was in pain. I remembered a fall on our driveway in which she had landed, literally, face first and had cried a lot. I had briefly worried about a broken nose, but she recovered within a few minutes and went back to playing. Perhaps that's when she broke her arm? We didn't know. Leah's arm was wrapped from hand to mid-upper arm in pink fiberglass.

On July 5 we were all in the living room, with me on the computer, Daniel reading, and Leah waltzing around with a piece of lavender gauzy material she was using as an accessory in some mysterious toddler dance. She stepped on the material while walking across our hardwood floors, her foot slipped, and I heard a clear snapping sound as she went down. A trip to the ER and an X-ray revealed a clean, nondisplaced fracture in the middle of her left tibia. For the next few weeks, Leah had matching pink casts on her left side, arm and leg. She was cast-free again by early August.

On August 30, three days before I was to start IVF, some friends were playing at our house. The kids had emptied the basket of books we kept in the living room, scattering the books around the room. Leah stepped on a book, which slid on the wood floor, causing her right leg to shoot out to the side. She made a choking half-cough, half-cry sound of surprise and pain, then began shrieking. I instinctively reached out and pulled her onto my lap; the movement made her shake spasmodically from head to toe. I realized, too late, that I should not have moved her at all. She continued to shake and scream, and soon her blond curls were plastered to her forehead with sweat. I called my mom, and together we managed to get Leah to the children's hospital ER. By the time we were settled into a treatment room, her right thigh had swollen up to twice its size.

Thank God for children's hospitals. They gave her morphine before the X-ray, and the X-ray tech refused to take more than one picture because it would require moving Leah and inflicting too much pain. One X-ray was enough to confirm a spiral fracture of the right femur, a split down most of the length of her bone. It was late on a Friday afternoon, and Leah's orthopedist, still in scrubs after a day of surgery, arrived with two residents and the cast technician (who somehow managed to have immaculate clothing all the time—stiff, spotless white shirts, sharply creased wool pants—despite spending all day with plaster and fiberglass casting material). They sedated Leah and gathered around her to get her into a hip spica cast. Frankly, we had had enough of pink fiberglass that summer, but now Leah was encased in it. The cast covered her whole right leg, her hips and torso up to her chest, plus half of her left leg.

We got home from the ER around nine that evening, settled Leah on the pull-out couch in our living room, and gave her something to eat, some pain reliever, and a sedative. But despite the drugs, every time she began drifting off to sleep, the muscles in her broken thigh would tense and she would startle awake, whimpering with pain. This went on for several hours. In the wee hours of the morning, I gave her another dose of sedative and stroked her hair until, finally, she fell asleep. Weary, wound up, and devastated, I was unable to sleep and instead wrote an e-mail to an OI parents' Listserv I was a part of, seeking solace and advice.

I was overwhelmed by feelings brought on by the proximity of Leah's fracture to the beginning of our IVF cycle in just three days. With the sharp-edged clarity that comes only in the depths of a sleepless night, I felt I could not possibly allow this agony another foothold in our family's life. Our lovely and beloved Leah had OI, and we would cope. Of course we would cope. But this pain of cracked bones, hoarse cries, and entire seasons stolen out from under us was no longer welcome. If we were to have another baby, he or she had to have strong bones.

We spent September caring for our injured child and going through the exhausting IVF process at the same time. The one advantage to this confluence of events was that I spent very little time worrying about whether the IVF cycle would work. I was too tired and preoccupied for anxiety. The last week in September, ultrasounds and blood tests revealed that my daily injections of ovary-stimulating hormones had worked, spurring my ovaries to produce multiple mature eggs instead of the single egg that matures during most normal menstrual cycles. The next step involved a new and more difficult type of injection. Until this point, all the injections had been subcutaneous (into the skin). I could give them to myself, using a very thin, short needle in the skin of my abdomen or thigh. Beyond a slight sting, it was not painful. The next round of medications, first to force my ovaries to release the mature eggs and then to prepare my uterine lining to receive embryos, had to be injected directly into a large muscle—my buttocks—by using a larger, longer needle. The night before my egg retrieval, at a precise time given to us by the Center, I lay on our couch, bare butt exposed. Daniel, with the help and advice of my mother (a nurse), plunged a needle in and injected a hormone that would cause my ovaries to release the mature eggs right at the time I was scheduled for retrieval the next day.

The following morning we went to the Center, where I was sedated and woke up a little later to learn that sixteen mature eggs had been retrieved from my ovaries. This seemed to be a good number; because I was only thirty-four years old, with no history of miscarriage or infertility, it was assumed that the eggs would be healthy and easily fertilized. I went home to recover on the couch, with a cup of Dunkin' Donuts coffee; caffeine was discouraged during an IVF cycle, but I had a reprieve that day because my eggs were out of me and an embryo was not yet in me. The lab went to work, injecting Daniel's sperm into each egg. The following day we learned that, for reasons no one could explain, only four of the fertilized eggs had developed. All our hopes lay in four little clusters of six to eight cells each. A cell was extracted from each fertilized egg and clearly labeled to keep track of which cell came from which egg. With an escort, these extracted cells were flown to Chicago, where a unique test had been developed specifically for my OI mutation. A few days later we learned that only one of the four had tested negative for OI. With only one embryo to transfer, at least I could stop worrying about a multiple pregnancy.

I had a one-day hiatus from medications after egg retrieval, but now Daniel was injecting me, still in the buttocks, with a viscous, oily concoction of progesterone to build up and maintain my uterine lining. I was to receive these injections daily until my pregnancy test, when we would learn whether to continue them (because I was pregnant) or stop them (because I was not). I developed a large, sore knot at the injection site that remained for months after the IVF cycle. A few days after beginning the progesterone shots, I returned to the Center to have our single embryo transferred, feeling very relaxed, thanks to a sedative that the Center routinely prescribes for the transfer procedure. The nurse told me that they started giving Valium when they found that some women were so nervous that their thighs had to be pried apart to allow the doctor to transfer embryos.

The doctor arrived with a picture of the embryo, which looked like a photo from my ninth-grade biology textbook, and said, "There's your baby." I was surprised by this little flash of humanity among all this technology and to-the-letter protocol. I wondered if I had misheard him. It seemed vaguely irresponsible to name this little cluster as our child, when we all knew that the chances of the cells developing into an actual baby were considerably less than the chances that they would fail to develop and be expelled with my next period.

The embryo transfer was straightforward and mildly uncomfortable, like an especially long pelvic exam. When I was discharged home for twenty-four hours of bed rest, a nurse went over everything I shouldn't do: I was not to lift, vacuum, exercise, or go up and down stairs except when absolutely necessary. She told us about one woman who went home after her transfer and painted her basement floor. Daniel asked if the woman's cycle had worked. The nurse shook her head and rolled her eyes, "Some people have more money than sense." I thought of the strung-out, confused woman who had arrived late to our IVF class months before.

We went home and we waited. We also started looking at houses, because Leah's fracture-filled summer revealed that our house, with six steps at the front entrance and the only bathroom on the second floor, was not well-suited for a family with two fragile-boned members. My pregnancy test was scheduled a little less than two weeks later, but I knew before then that the cycle had failed. I lay in bed at night, fingering my breasts, looking for some sign of tenderness or swelling that might indicate pregnancy. But they were as tiny and unremarkable as always.

My pregnancy test was on a Wednesday morning. I went to the Center, gave my vial of blood, then went home and waited in our bedroom. The hopeful energy of the room's pale blue, spring-sky walls was powerless against the October chill and my resigned preoccupation with the news to come. Finally the phone rang: the nurse in charge of our cycle told me that the test was negative. No more progesterone injections for me. And no baby. She told me to call her in a few weeks if we wanted to try again. We could start another cycle around the New Year, which would give us a few months for my body to recover and to celebrate the holidays without the daily pressures of an IVF cycle.

The Market Orientation of Fertility Medicine

The *New York Times* contributing writer Peggy Orenstein's memoir about infertility, *Waiting for Daisy*, includes some raw observations about fertility clinic culture. After going through an unsuccessful IVF cycle that was characterized by poor communication among the clinic staff and between staff and patient, Orenstein

> felt like the high roller whose new friends disappeared when his stake was gone. The caring brochures, the chummy smiles, the warm affect of the clinic "team" seemed abruptly stripped away, revealing nothing more than a cold-blooded business. We had wanted so desperately to believe that we had ignored the sales pitch in the compassion, the coercion in the photographs of babies and sunflowers. But I finally got it—these guys may have been doctors, but they were also salesmen. I may have been a patient, but I was also a consumer. I was undergoing a procedure, but I was also making a deal—and they were making a buck.

Although doctors in many disciplines operate their practices as businesses and make good money, fertility clinics have a market orientation that sets them apart. Economist Debora Spar has observed that the fertility business, more so than other medical specialties, is ruled by the laws of supply and demand. The costs of treatment remain high in part because there are so many people willing to pay whatever it takes to conceive a baby, and there are a limited number of clinics with the technology to help them.

Recent deliberation on the high rate of multiple births after fertility treatment illustrates well the market pressures on both fertility clinicians and their patients. Recognizing that pregnancies with more than one baby can lead to significant health risks for both mothers and babies, the American Society for Reproductive Medicine adopted voluntary guidelines for clinicians in 2009. These guidelines recommend the number of embryos to be transferred based on the woman's age and assessment of various conditions such as embryo quality and the success rate of previous IVF cycles. For example, the guidelines recommend that women under thirty-five receive only one embryo or, under some circumstances, no more than two. However, according to the *New York Times*,

> Many fertility doctors routinely ignore their industry's own guidelines, which encourage the use of single embryos during the in-vitro fertilization procedure, according to interviews and industry data. Some doctors say that powerful financial incentives hold sway in a competitive marketplace. Placing extra embryos in a woman's womb increases the chances that one will take. The resulting babies and word of mouth can be the best way of luring new business.
>
> Doctors are also often under pressure from patients eager for children, who have incentives to gamble as well. Frequently, they have come to IVF as a last resort after years of other treatments, are paying out of pocket, and are anxious to be successful on the first try.

As of this writing, only fifteen states mandate insurance coverage for fertility treatment, and some of those do not require insurance companies to cover the most expensive techniques, such as IVF. That leaves prospective parents paying as much as ten to fifteen thousand dollars out of pocket for each cycle of IVF or PGD, and they often go through multiple cycles before becoming pregnant or deciding to forgo further treatment. Although our nation's health insurance system is certainly not free of market considerations, the lack of insurance involvement in fertility medicine makes financial considerations more obvious and straightforward than in most medical disciplines: For patients to obtain treatment, they must pay for it. They choose clinics and treatments that offer the most bang for their buck (that promise the highest likelihood of success). For clinics to make money, they need to attract patients with money to spend. To attract more patients, they need to show results.

Institutions are clearly aware that fertility medicine is a lucrative business that can be good for their bottom line. For example, a 2009 study of university salaries by the *Chronicle of Higher*

Education revealed that fertility specialists were among the highest paid employees of large universities with associated medical centers, in some cases earning salaries of two or three million dollars a year, more than their university presidents. These salaries are not typical; the American Medical Group Association's annual salary survey lists reproductive endocrinologists as earning an average of $317,312 per year (2006 data). But the existence of multimillion dollar salaries for some high-profile fertility specialists shows that organizations put a high value on fertility medicine's contributions to their institutions' financial health.

Clinics and patients are not the only stakeholders in the big business of making babies. Sperm donors, egg donors, and surrogates are all compensated for their contributions to conception and birth. Compensation for egg donors and surrogates has typically raised more concerns than that for sperm donors, because the risks women face in egg donation, pregnancy, and birth make these endeavors more prone to troubling scenarios in which women risk their health because they need the money. As with multiple embryo transfers, voluntary guidelines have failed to quiet many of those concerns. For example, while the American Society for Reproductive Medicine recommends that egg donors receive no more than $5,000 in compensation, a 2010 Hastings Center report showed that recruitment ads aimed at college women regularly offered more than $5,000 (occasionally as much as $50,000) for donated eggs, and that higher compensation was offered at colleges where students have higher SAT scores.

Anything Goes—Except When It Doesn't

Clinicians' uneven adherence to voluntary guidelines on embryo transfers and egg-donor compensation reveals another defining characteristic of American fertility medicine compared to other nations: it is largely unregulated. The result is that fertility medicine is not only driven largely by market dynamics but also operates in an environment where technological innovations become available before practitioners, patients, government, and the public can consider the cultural and moral questions raised by those innovations. Clinics are free to provide whatever services are technically possible, so long as people are willing to pay for them. This system leads to periodic public outcries when clinics cross a line into questionable ethical territory, although to be fair to clinicians, the public has done a poor job of deciding, or even discussing, where those lines should lie.

For example, in early 2009 Doctor Jeffrey Steinberg of the Los Angeles-based Fertility Institutes announced that his clinic would allow patients to use PGD to select not only for gender (a service his clinic has offered for several years) but also for cosmetic traits including eye and hair color. The clinic decided to postpone offering this service indefinitely due to an overwhelmingly negative reaction, including statements from other PGD practitioners who insisted that the technology was designed for and should be limited to ensuring the health of babies at risk for genetic disorders. This controversy illustrates journalist Liza Mundy's observation about the anything-goes market orientation of reproductive medicine: "What is at work in assisted reproduction is often not science but business . . . commercialization does make some clinics far too willing to offer patients an array of services whose implications and consequences are often not spelled out or even understood, really, by anybody."

Mundy traces the experimental, unregulated nature of U.S. reproductive medicine to the 1995 passage of the Dickey-Wicker Amendment, a rider on a Congressional appropriations bill that prohibited use of federal funds either to create embryos for the purpose of scientific research or to conduct any research on embryos that would result in the embryos' destruction. Although this legislation is most frequently cited in discussions of stem cell research, it also "meant that no federally funded experiments could be conducted on the safety and efficacy of IVF" and associated techniques. By banning federal funding of embryo research, the government in effect removed itself from involvement in the evolution of fertility medicine. As a result, fertility clinicians operate under voluntary rather than mandated guidelines, and developments in fertility science and practice come not from the lab, but from the clinic. Improvements making IVF safer and more effective—such as guidelines on the number of embryos to transfer or recent research that helps doctors predict whether a second IVF cycle will succeed based on data from the first—have come about through experience with actual patients

whose treatments, conceptions, and pregnancies are studied to determine what works and what doesn't.

The unregulated U.S. fertility medicine market stands in contrast with highly regulated European systems. Although America
is more socially conservative than Europe, and Americans report
a higher level of religious belief than Europeans do, U.S. fertility
clinics operate with fewer constraints than European clinics. Some
European countries completely ban certain procedures, such as IVF
and PGD. A German court made headlines in the summer of 2010
when it acquitted a doctor charged with performing illegal abortion
after he had used PGD on several embryos (the doctor's actions had
been equated with abortion and counted as violating laws that protect embryos). News accounts surmised that the court decision will
probably lead Germany to tighten laws banning PGD. The British
regulatory system is perhaps the most relevant for Americans; as in
the United States, IVF and PGD are both legal in Britain. However,
the procedures are overseen by a government agency, the Human
Fertilisation and Embryology Authority (HFEA). The HFEA creates
and oversees guidelines on fertility medicine, including specifying
the genetic disorders for which it is legal to test via PGD and determining how much compensation egg donors can receive. Regulation,
while solving some problems (no British clinic is going to advertise
PGD for eye-color selection), raises others. Egg donors, for example,
can only be reimbursed for certain expenses, not paid a fee. As a
result, British fertility clinics have access to far fewer donor eggs
than American clinics, leading some British women to come to the
United States for IVF with donor eggs. This is just one example of
a growing trade in "fertility tourism"—a phenomenon that lays bare
the market orientation of reproductive medicine.

A Whole New Way to Bring Home Baby

In June 2010 channel HBO2 aired a documentary titled *Google Baby*
about the growing practice of couples from developed countries—
including the United States, Britain, and Israel—who hire Indian
women to serve as surrogates for their IVF-conceived babies, often
using donor sperm and/or donor eggs. Several Indian fertility clinics

conduct every step of the process: They market their services to pro-spective clients (including travel services so that the parents-to-be can sightsee while they are in India to participate in an IVF cycle or retrieve their new baby); recruit surrogates, usually low-income Indian women with several children of their own; help clients obtain donor gametes when needed; perform IVF; house, feed, and provide medical care to surrogates for the entire length of their pregnancies; and deliver babies. As of this writing, the Indian government is con-sidering more oversight of these practices, including separating the various steps so that the organizations matching parents with surro-gates are not also performing IVF.

Google Baby made for troubling TV, and several scenes have stayed with me. In one scene, an Indian woman who recently gave birth to a baby destined for a foreign couple sits by her husband as he talks about his wife's surrogacy. Their own big-eyed, beauti-ful little boy—who appeared in a previous scene while visiting his pregnant mother as she lived apart from her family in a special house for surrogate mothers—plays nearby. The husband talks about the difference their surrogate payment has made, allowing them to buy a house and other comforts. He says that he expects his wife will serve as a surrogate again in the future and adds that, although women's brains are generally inferior to men's, his wife made a good deci-sion when she agreed to be a surrogate. The wife, who admitted in an earlier scene that handing the baby over right after birth was very painful, listens in silence.

In another disturbing exchange, an Israeli entrepreneur named Doron—who started a business of connecting egg donors, sperm donors, aspiring parents, and Indian clinics after becoming a parent through surrogacy himself—is on the phone, talking to a prospec-tive father. Doron tells the client that the Indian clinic has suggested implanting two separate embryos in two different surrogates, to increase the chances of a successful pregnancy. This might mean that the client will end up with twins born of two different moth-ers. If either of the embryos divides into twins or if several embryos are transferred into either woman and more than one implants, the client could even end up with three or four children. The cli-ent doesn't hesitate to accept this plan and, amid chuckles over the idea of all those babies, mentions that selective reduction (aborting one or more embryos in a multiple pregnancy) has always been an acceptable option anyway. After hanging up, Doron mentions that he feels uncomfortable with this decision even though everyone else involved seems to be on board. But, he adds, maybe he just needs a little time to get used to the idea of using two surrogates.

Finally, in a scene I can't put out of my mind, an Indian woman is on the operating table, giving birth to a baby via C-section. She says that she can feel the doctor cutting, and it becomes clear that her anesthesia is not working properly. The anesthesiologist puts something into her IV line, and soon she is lying still, awake but heavily sedated. One doctor standing by her head pushes hard on her belly over and over, as if he is kneading a particularly stubborn loaf of bread, while another doctor pulls the baby out. Immediately after delivering the baby, the doctor answers a cell-phone call while a clinic staff person wraps the baby and takes her away. The baby's intended parents' travel schedule will not bring them to India to pick up their baby for several days, so in the meantime, the staffer will care for the infant. The surrogate lies on a stretcher, her eyes dazed and vacant, as her husband holds her hand and strokes her hair.

That last scene hit me particularly hard because one of my C-sections also involved a failed epidural and the administration of drugs that did not completely abolish the pain but helped me to mentally check out enough that I no longer cared. It was one of the more harrowing experiences of my life. But at least when it was over, I could see my husband holding a tiny yellow-hatted bundle, and I knew that I had a baby whom I could soon hold and nurse. That Indian surrogate had no such solace. And the baby herself was adrift, in the temporary care of a professional until her parents arrived to claim the infant they had paid thousands of dollars for—although many fewer thousands than they would have paid for the same procedure in the United States or Europe. A baby had been born, an event that usually brings people together. But all the parties involved ended up essentially alone, disconnected from each other and from the central event of a baby's birth: The doctor takes a phone call, the surrogate woozily recovers from sedation, the intended parents make travel plans, and the baby is whisked away.

India is not the only destination for fertility tourism. The difference in compensation for American and British egg donors means that British women travel to the United States for IVF treatment, so they can gain access to the large pool of U.S. egg donors. Guatemalan women are being recruited as surrogate mothers in a small but growing industry, similar to that in India. Fertility tourism illustrates that while some fertility patients will do just about anything to fulfill their desire for a baby, they are not immune to cost considerations. If they can access the same services—donor gametes, IVF, surrogacy—at a lower price, then some of them will.

What Are We Trying to Do Again?

Some writers concerned about the ethics of assisted reproduction have pointed out that the arrangements common in fertility tourism (although they happen in the United States as well)—in which babies are conceived with *both* donor eggs and donor sperm, not just one or the other, and gestated by a surrogate—are really not that different from adoption of infants. Though I objected to the overused question "Why don't you just adopt?" in an earlier chapter, this question is a valid one to ask in response to complex arrangements in which parents bring home babies unconnected to them by either genetics or biology (gestation and birth). When parents eager to have a baby of their own end up paying thousands of dollars for donor sperm *and* donor eggs *and* a gestational surrogate, it raises the question of why a genetically unrelated baby born via surrogate is preferable to a genetically unrelated baby available for adoption. Perhaps prospective parents prefer the control (or the illusion of control) that is possible when they can select donors and surrogates who meet certain criteria and can obtain a baby on their own schedule rather than enduring the long waits associated with some types of adoptions. Perhaps it also reflects how easily we can become blind to some central truths of parenting (that no parents can dictate what kind of child they get, for example) when we are immersed in a medical specialty whose success is measured by its "take-home baby" rate and where clinicians stand ready to help parents conceive children by using almost any technological means.

Once again Peggy Orenstein provides a biting assessment of clinical culture, pointing out how easily fertility clinics' definition of

success changes, based on which treatments work and which ones
don't. "What was with these guys?" Orenstein wondered when her
doctor explained why IVF with a donor egg was a better option after
IVF with her own eggs failed.

[The doctors] dangled IVF in front of us and *after* it failed—
and we'd shelled out the cash—said I was a bad candidate for it.
What's more, after implying that a genetic link to our baby was
so important that it was worth going to physical and financial
strains to attain, they whipped around and implied that the link,
at least my link, was no big deal: the key to motherhood was
carrying the child, not conceiving it. I wondered whether, if my
problem had been a wonky uterus, he'd be insinuating that the
vessel didn't matter—anyone could grow a baby—it was the egg
that made the mom.

Once prospective parents have stepped through the doors of a
fertility clinic, they have entered a realm in which medical providers often assume that patients will do whatever it takes, at whatever
cost, with whatever technology is available, to eventually bring a baby
home. As ethicist Paul Lauritzen has observed, "Infertility specialists
simply assume that individuals will pursue all possible treatments.
. . . The very availability of the technology appears to exert a sort of
tyrannical pressure to use it." And it is not only medical providers'
assumptions that dictate the process, but patients' adoption of similar
assumptions, which makes clearheaded choices increasingly difficult
as patients become more and more immersed in the clinical culture.
Lauritzen observes: "Once one has become goal oriented in the process of reproduction, choices about interventions tend to get framed
exclusively in terms of the likelihood of the intervention successfully
realizing the goal of producing a healthy child. . . . Once one has,
so to speak, relinquished one's gametes to the doctors in order to
achieve the goal of conception, it becomes difficult to judge various
technological manipulations . . . by criteria other than the likelihood
of success." It becomes increasingly difficult to step back and ask
whether trying the next promising technology makes sense—logi-
cally, financially, morally, emotionally. It can feel impossible to step
off the fertility-treatment treadmill. After all, what if the *next* treatment is the one that works?

Clinical Attitudes toward Genetic Disorders

This chapter has thus far focused on issues raised by fertility medicine in general, and especially IVF. But many prospective parents, including Daniel and me, encounter reproductive medicine not primarily because they cannot conceive but because they have the potential to conceive a child with a genetic disorder. Like us, they may explore PGD to ensure that a future child does not inherit a genetic anomaly, or they may face decisions concerning prenatal diagnosis: whether to undergo prenatal testing, which techniques to use, and what to do with the information that results. Many people in these situations report encountering a medical culture that holds outdated, pessimistic, or incomplete perceptions of what it is like to raise a child with a genetic disorder.

The media and advocates for people with disabilities have given much attention to studies showing that termination rates for fetuses prenatally diagnosed with Down syndrome are around 90 percent. (This does not mean that 90 percent of babies with Down syndrome are aborted because not all cases are prenatally diagnosed.) Studies by Brian Skotko, MD, "found that expectant mothers who received a prenatal diagnosis [of Down syndrome] felt their physicians provided them with incomplete, inaccurate, and oftentimes offensive information about the condition. Other studies have shown physicians themselves feeling unprepared and uninformed to deliver a diagnosis." Many of the parents interviewed felt their experience of prenatal diagnosis would have been better if doctors offered more up-to-date information about Down syndrome and referral to support groups. Instead, many parents report that doctors and genetic counselors emphasize the option to terminate the pregnancy, paint a bleak picture of life with Down syndrome, and fail to either inform patients about medical advances and community resources that have improved the prognosis for many affected people or refer them to families who could provide firsthand accounts of life with Down syndrome.

When theologian Brian Brock and his wife, Stephanie, had a child with Down syndrome, they encountered a medical system (in Europe) that made assumptions about both what parents want to know and what parents would do with that information. When the Brocks went to the clinic during what appeared to be a normal pregnancy with a healthy baby to ask about "antenatal care and birth arrangements," they were offered a sonogram for the purpose of determining the baby's conception date and gestational age in case they decided to abort. "This became our first experience of being offered medical treatment which we neither sought nor desired," the Brocks recall, "but were subjected to as a feature of the institutional, legal and social location of women's medicine." When, after their son's birth, the Brocks learned that he likely had Down syndrome, they refused genetic testing to confirm the diagnosis. The testing was offered not only to help them plan for their son's care but also to make clear whether they would need genetic testing in future pregnancies, because the medical system seemed to assume that they would not want to have additional such children. The Brocks go on to assert that "simply *having* genetic testing has shifted medical behavior toward the disabled," although they concede that many medical professionals disagree with that assessment, saying that prenatal testing is offered without judgment of what should be done with the information the testing provides.

Amy Julia Becker went into her second and third pregnancies expecting some pressure from her medical providers to do extensive prenatal testing because her first child was born with Down syndrome. Becker is troubled by many doctors' attitude toward prenatal diagnosis, which assumes that parents need to know if something is wrong so that they can choose whether or not to terminate, and that parents who have one child with a genetic disorder will naturally want to prevent having another one. But she also understands where those attitudes might come from. In their medical training, doctors often see only the sickest or most disabled children and thus have a skewed perception of the suffering that comes along with certain disabilities and diagnoses.

This skewed perception can be a problem when severe OI is prenatally diagnosed, often due to fractures and bone deformities being apparent on routine ultrasounds. Because OI is a relatively rare disorder, many physicians have not encountered anyone with it and will only recall a textbook photo or description of severe or fatal forms of OI. Many physicians are unaware of the broad spectrum of severity that occurs in OI, as well as new drug treatments and surgical techniques that have improved mobility, fracture recovery times, and activity level for many children, even in severe cases. Though it's possible to diagnose severe OI prenatally, it is difficult to know the exact extent of severity before birth. I suddenly lost my appetite one Sunday morning in 2005 when I read a *New York Times Magazine* "Lives" column written by a young father whose baby was prenatally diagnosed with OI. The doctor declared with certainty that the baby had the most severe form of OI, Type II, which is always fatal within hours, days, or months of birth. The father wrote:

> You know you've arrived in a different universe when the word "fatal" comes as a relief. Because until that moment, I had been trying to extrapolate what the flesh-and-blood version of this baby would look like in the maple crib we'd ordered, asking myself if we had it in us to raise such a severely compromised baby. Liz would later tell me that she was also sadly relieved. "Fatal" was our absolution—we would not have to learn darker truths about ourselves.

I lost my appetite not because I blamed this young couple for making such a harrowing decision, but because I knew there was a chance their doctor was wrong about the "fatal" part of his diagnosis. It is not always possible to clearly differentiate between fatal OI and severe OI in utero. I know more than one family who received a prenatal diagnosis of fatal OI, carried the pregnancy to term, gathered loved ones to say good-bye to their baby within hours of birth, and today are parents of teenagers and young adults who have had many fractures and surgeries yet are very much alive. Perhaps this young couple's doctor was right, or perhaps he made a bad diagnosis based on limited information about and experience with OI.

Journalist Melanie Phillips, in an editorial criticizing Doctor Robert Edwards's statement that "soon it will be a 'sin'" to have babies with genetic disorders, wrote that physicians' pessimistic attitudes toward genetic disorders and bias toward pregnancy termination are often "motivated simply by compassion to prevent suffering. They observe in their clinics the agonies of patients and their families and seek as a result to prevent such grief and distress from happening in the first place. However," Phillips continued, "such a commendable attitude shades quickly into arrogance, a lack of humility in the face of human resilience and tenacity. There is also a shocking refusal to accept that gravely disabled people can experience happiness or bring it to others." Clinicians' focus on preventing suffering forms the basis of a classic ethical argument in favor of using PGD to prevent genetic disorders.

PGD as Primary Preventive Medicine

Journalist Liza Mundy has pointed out that PGD is often used by families who are at risk of having babies with genetic disorders but who don't want to undergo prenatal diagnosis because they would never choose pregnancy termination. Prospective parents are not alone in perceiving PGD as morally preferable to pregnancy termination after prenatal diagnosis. Two physicians who helped develop PGD techniques, Yuri Verlinsky and Anver Kuliev, make the same argument in their classic textbook on PGD, in which they label the technique as "primary preventive medicine," similar to public health initiatives such as increased folic acid intake for pregnant women. These various preventive measures "are ethically acceptable in any population, because they provide the actual gain in infants free of congenital malformations rather than the avoidance of birth of affected children." Verlinsky and Kuliev point out that PGD and other preventive measures are "better tolerated by society" than pregnancy termination.

This lumping of PGD in with other preventive measures for ensuring the birth of healthy babies is both very understandable and somewhat troubling. Certainly Daniel and I would never terminate a pregnancy if prenatal diagnosis revealed that the baby had OI, yet we willingly underwent PGD. We perceived a difference between choosing to discard an affected embryo and choosing to abort an affected fetus. But is there really a difference? Certainly those who claim full human status for embryos from the moment of conception, such as the Roman Catholic Church and many pro-life organizations and individuals, would say there is no difference; just because it is emotionally easier for parents to reject a six-cell embryo than to abort a recognizably human fetus does not make it morally superior.

Author Masha Gessen, who in her book *Blood Matters* chronicled her examination of modern genetic medicine after she learned that she was genetically predisposed to breast cancer, observes that "it is far easier for humans, whatever their ethical and religious beliefs, to reject embryos than to abort fetuses." Gessen criticizes and ultimately rejects ethical arguments against PGD in favor of recognizing the emotional nature of parents' decisions as valid and appropriate. In her view, "the clinical sterility of such discussions [over the ethics of PGD] is a luxury compared with the human torment geneticists witnessed, sometimes experienced, and often tried to alleviate back in the days of prenatal testing."

PGD pioneers Verlinsky and Kuliev are likewise sympathetic to families' emotional responses to difficult circumstances; they go a step further to say that PGD is the responsible choice for such families to make: "The extremely difficult life experience of families affected by any catastrophic early- or late-onset inherited disorder, of seeing suffering from the disease and being anxious that they themselves will be soon affected, makes them responsible to ensure that future generations will not be faced with the same difficulties." Verlinsky and Kuliev also argue that in assisted reproduction, embryos are routinely assessed by "morphological criteria, which has the goal of identifying the embryos with the highest developmental potential. PGD . . . allows improvement of the embryo selection, by applying genetic tests. . . . In other words, the advent of PGD is a natural evolution of assisted reproduction."

Making People Better or Making Better People?

As someone interested in hearing, responding to, and honoring people's stories, including their subjective and emotional responses to their and their children's suffering, I think there is some merit to the argument that PGD is preventive medicine. I support the national OI Foundation, which names a cure for the disorder among its goals—a goal I share. How are we to cure a genetic disorder without eliminating or altering the genes that cause it? Perhaps one day we'll be able to alter the genes of living, breathing people affected by genetic disorders (and such alterations will certainly raise ethical concerns of their own), but for now, PGD offers one way of freeing families from the legacy of genetic disease.

However, I think arguments naming PGD as preventive medicine are oversimplified, ignoring questions, particularly relevant for people of faith, about how far it is appropriate for us to go in altering some fundamental truths of human identity: Our bodies are limited and fallible. We get hurt, we sicken, and we die. Sometimes fullness of life happens in spite of or even because of great suffering. Ultimately we are not in charge of our (or our children's) lives, and that can be a good thing. As theologian Stanley Hauerwas has said, "The ability of modern medicine to cure is at once a benefit and a potential pitfall. Too often it is tempted to increase its power by offering more than care, by offering in fact alleviation from the human condition."

The troubling aspect of PGD is that, in trying to eliminate children's suffering, we eliminate the children, or at least the embryos that will become children. We potentially foster medical and cultural attitudes that classify certain people as undesirable, reducing the fullness of human identity to a list of good versus bad traits. Clinicians involved in reproductive medicine potentially end up reinforcing damaging cultural norms rather than simply providing care. In her editorial on Doctor Edwards's infamous remark that it will soon be a "sin" to bear genetically disabled children, journalist Melanie Phillips worried that clinicians will come to believe "that there are standards by which some lives can be judged to be worthless and that science makes a better judge than an emotional mother." She went on to say that Edwards's remark "was a remarkable moral inversion that turned eugenic arguments, which should be seen as a blot on our humanity, into a social good and made a sinner of anyone who did not practice them. Apart from a lamentable moral deficiency, this also displayed a distinct lack of scientific imagination, since genetic normality is surely a contradiction in terms. Who can be said to be 'normal'? We are each of us, after all, unique."

Brian and Stephanie Brock, parents of a child with Down syndrome, have observed that "contemporary medicine finds itself in a framework of fear rather than gratitude, and so finds it difficult to separate medicine as a project responsible for creating 'normal' children from medicine as a human technique for caring for each person's physical problems." Other theologians and ethicists have explained this modern medical dilemma by emphasizing the difference between "care" (providing treatment that alleviates suffering and allows people to live as full a life as possible) and "cure" (fixing what's wrong). Certainly medicine is often able to cure what ails us. The potential problem comes when medicine is used not to cure only ailments but also to cure the human condition, which includes qualities (dependence, diversity, and limitation, for example) that can cause suffering but also add necessary richness.

The tricky part, for me at least, is to figure out when medical cures should be welcomed and when medicine goes too far in altering the human condition. Using PGD with the goal of eliminating OI in a family can be perceived simply as good medicine, an assurance that no one in that family ever need worry again about snapping a bone after a routine fall. And it can also be perceived as a vain attempt to fix things that are ultimately unfixable, and that perhaps should not be fixed—the limitations that can reveal what is most valuable in life (which is not perfect, beautiful, and unfailingly strong bodies). I'm not sure how to judge which perception is more accurate, but I'm convinced that we need to keep examining the perceptions anyway.

Questions to Think About

1. How does fertility medicine—its assumptions, purposes, and operating principles—differ from other medical specialties? Are those differences cause for concern?
2. Is it reasonable to classify PGD as primary preventive medicine? Is there a moral difference between discarding embryos affected by a genetic disorder and aborting a fetus with the same disorder?
3. How might we assess when medicine goes too far in trying to "cure" the human condition? Or is eliminating dependence, limitation, and physical and emotional suffering a reasonable goal for modern medicine?
4. What resources might help patients be better equipped to evaluate the services offered by reproductive medicine and make informed choices about what treatments to consent to?

What Is Lost along the Way

Reflections on Embryos

We'll never know why the single embryo we had transferred failed to implant and develop. As for the other three fertilized eggs—the ones that tested positive for OI—we had them discarded. Destroyed. At the time, in the emotional muddle of caring for a broken toddler while involved in a medical process loaded with questions that were at best complex and at worst unanswerable, I thought little of those embryos. Even the other embryo, the one that was transferred, took up little space in my imagination. I was so tired, confused, and sad. I got us through each day, focused solely on the tasks necessary to care for my family, and that was all I could do.

After the transfer procedure, I had done everything I was supposed to do. I rested, avoided caffeine and alcohol, and tried to avoid stress. But we were looking for a new house, one meeting our very specific needs for accessibility (e.g., no more than one step at the front door, a bathroom on the main floor, a relatively flat yard). The day after our embryo transfer, after the twenty-four-hour enforced rest period was done, I went to a real estate open house. I came home agitated, anxious, and weepy because the house I visited seemed perfect for us, but our agent hadn't told us about it, and now there were already multiple offers. Eventually, after strained conversations with our agent and her calls to the listing agent, we learned that we never would have had a chance anyway. A bidding war drove up the price higher than what we could afford.

When I received the negative pregnancy test results two weeks later, I refused to participate in any kind of "What if . . ." blame-game stuff. But in researching and writing this book, I have thought more about the embryo that was transferred and then lost, and have even indulged a few "What if . . ." scenarios. What if I hadn't gone to that open house? What if I had stayed in bed, curled myself tightly around that small life inside and protected it? Sometimes I think I should have honored that life more than I did, although it probably would not have made a difference. With all our advances in science, no one has yet figured out what makes some embryos implant and thrive, and some wither and die. Fertility doctors try to choose fertilized eggs that appear healthy and robust, but there are no foolproof methods for predicting whether even the healthiest-looking embryos will grow into babies.

That Wednesday afternoon when I learned that our PGD cycle had failed, I cried a little but otherwise spared few emotions for the negative test. The disappointment, while sharp, was also expected. I didn't have the time or energy to grieve. The following day, Leah's hip spica cast came off, and the relief of that occasion, along with my fervent house hunting, distracted me from our failure. We would try again in January; in the meantime, I had a little girl who needed help in getting back on her feet, and we had a quest to find a house that would give both of us more freedom.

In November we found a small one-story home that suited our needs, so we put our house on the market. The real estate market in our town was booming, and we priced our house at $60,000 more than we had paid for it just two years before. After using part of the profit for a down payment on our new house, we would have enough left to pay off the remaining bills from our first PGD cycle and pay for another. We received two offers on our house the first day it was on the market.

By Christmas, Leah was sporting a new pair of lightweight plastic ankle braces to correct her severely flattened feet (she walked more on her instep than on her soles) and, fully recovered from the femur fracture, was walking more steadily than ever before. In January she would begin preschool at a town-sponsored program that integrated children who qualified for special education (which Leah did) with typically developing children. November and December were busy with medical and school appointments, lining up a mortgage for our new house, and holiday preparations. But PGD was still on our minds. We planned to try again but were frustrated by having to wait until the new year; the Center closed for a month starting in early December for updating of equipment and to give the staff a break from the precision timing of IVF cycles over the holidays. In late December I called our nurse to let her know my period had started, which would determine when in January we could begin our next cycle. I was stunned when she told me we'd have to wait until February. Their schedule was overflowing, and it would be too difficult to fit us in.

Then financial worries surfaced again. The buyers of our house backed out of the deal the day after Christmas, and we put the house back on the market during the Christmas–New Year real estate lull, in the midst of a series of early winter snowstorms. We had few showings and no offers.

I felt increasingly uncertain about whether trying another PGD cycle was the right decision. We didn't know how we would pay for it. Our house would eventually sell, but would we get the profit we had anticipated? I was frustrated that we had to conceive our child on someone else's schedule, especially when I knew we could conceive on our own if we wished. Much like the woman who missed the first half of our introductory IVF class, I had adopted the mind-set of a customer who becomes disgruntled when a service provider can't deliver what I want when I want it.

Yet I was also very aware that the Center was not merely a business to provide a service or product. It was involved in an endeavor that engaged body, mind, and soul and that raised vital questions about human identity and the promise and limits of medical technology. So I was frustrated as well that the Center's system largely failed to acknowledge or accommodate those questions, treating us as mere customers, waiting in line until it was our turn to be served. As kind and competent as most of the Center staff were, I hated that they had so much power over our family, to dictate when our child's conception could occur, even though we had granted them that power. I hated that the decisions we had agonized over in deciding whether and how to have a second child meant nothing to them, that we were just another case that needed to be squeezed into their schedule.

In the midst of so much change at home, I was also weary at the thought of once again taking on the burdensome chores of IVF—the injections, blood tests, ultrasounds, and phone calls. I finally asked myself how I would feel if a second PGD cycle failed, after all of this. I realized that if it failed, I would want to try to conceive a baby on our own. I asked myself which scenario would grieve me more: never having another baby (if the second cycle failed and we didn't do another) or having two children with OI. The answer was suddenly clear: I wanted another baby no matter what his or her bones were like. The grief and fear that had kept me up the night after Leah's femur fracture, certain that I could not possibly go through this with another child, had faded. I could handle a second fragile baby, as hard as it would be. I did not want to handle the prospect of never having another baby at all because we feared OI too much.

Around this time, our genetic counselor called and asked if I'd be willing to talk with a young woman and her husband who were exploring PGD for a genetic disorder that, like OI, was dominantly inherited. On a slushy January day, I dropped Leah off at preschool and met the couple, Renee and Steve,* at a Starbucks in town. Renee had a genetic disorder that caused some mild deformities and a speech impediment. Like me, she was the first in her family to have this disorder, but because it was caused by a dominant gene, her children had a 50 percent chance of inheriting it. On one of their first visits to our mutual genetic counselor, they learned that her disorder, if passed on to a child, could range widely in severity. Their child could have a fairly mild form of the disorder, requiring some therapy and minor reconstructive surgery, or the child could have significant cognitive and physical disabilities. When they learned that PGD was a possibility for them, Renee and Steve were overjoyed. They wondered why PGD wasn't talked about more frequently as a solution to genetic disease. "Here," they said, "is a tool that can help end the suffering of millions of children. Isn't that great? Why don't more people know about this? Why don't more people do this?"

I was sympathetic to their argument, having spent months chasing after this attractive solution to my own family's suffering. But given my growing uncertainty about trying another PGD cycle, I was unable to echo their enthusiasm. I kept my ruminations to myself and just shared with Renee and Steve the nuts and bolts of our experience—the procedures, the costs, the frustrations of working with

*Not their real names.

a clinical staff who, nice as they were, were caught up in a huge moneymaking venture. Rather than feeling connected to this couple because of our common experience, I felt disconnected as it dawned on me that, even leaving aside our emotional exhaustion and precarious finances, I wasn't sure I could continue with PGD. As I talked to Renee and Steve, my gut was saying that children, children like my fragile Leah, are gifts to be graciously accepted. As Renee and Steve extolled PGD's potential to end children's suffering, I kept thinking that the alleviation of suffering—even the suffering of children—is not the primary or sole measure of sound decisions.

But while I couldn't echo Renee and Steve's enthusiasm for PGD as a panacea for the suffering of sick children, I also couldn't say that PGD is always wrong, that those who employ PGD are always treating children as commodities rather than gifts. In 2004, long after Daniel and I had made our decisions about how to have a second child, *60 Minutes* did a piece on PGD in which they profiled two families. One used PGD to conceive triplets after their firstborn son died of spinal muscular atrophy as an infant. The other used PGD for sex selection because they wanted to have a girl after having several boys. The former evoked my empathy; the latter did not. Watching the first family cradle their healthy triplets seemed right and just and good. I would guess that they understand more than most parents just how much of a gift children are—both those who die after a brief and pain-filled life, and those who are robust and rosy cheeked. In a case such as theirs, it feels cruel to criticize PGD as a vain attempt to mold children to fit self-centered parental desires. Perhaps PGD can also be a way for people who have suffered unbearable losses to have a second chance, to move out from under the dead weight of grief and know the freedom of having children whose bodies do what they are supposed to do. God is with us in our suffering, but God is also present in the angry cries of a healthy newborn baby and in the tearful gratitude of parents who once wondered if they would spend the rest of their lives fingering the hole in their hearts, the one that will never, ever heal.

Our reasons for PGD fell somewhere between those of the parents whose baby died and those of the gender-balancing family; OI would not kill our children, but using genetic screening to protect a child from dozens of painful fractures is a bit more compelling than using it because you've always dreamed of having a little girl.

After going through one PGD cycle, we now knew how exhausting and unreliable the PGD process really is. Daniel's fatigue and frustration with the process mirrored mine in many ways, but we did not go so far as to call the Center and tell them we were done. Leah started school, we moved in mid-January, and we still hadn't sold our house, so it was easy to push a concrete decision about PGD to the back burner. But on one of our first nights in our new house, Daniel suggested that I skip my ritual trip to the bathroom for the birth control. That choice felt both reckless and necessary, like opening all the windows and doors on a frigid, gray winter's day and letting the wind rip through. My need to breathe in great gulps of fresh air trumped my fear that the gusts would tear apart the orderly world I was so desperately trying to construct.

After that night, I stopped thinking much about PGD because I had a gut feeling that I was pregnant. By the end of January, I was so sure that I went out and bought a buy-one-get-one-free pregnancy test kit. I took the first test and it was negative. Days passed. I continued to be sure that the pregnancy test was wrong and equally sure that I was an idiot for believing so. But I was addicted to peeing on a stick, so I took out the second test and tried again. I peed. I put the stick on the vanity next to the toilet. I waited a minute or two and looked. No pink line. I cursed myself under my breath, "Ellen, you fool. A waste of time and money." I went to wash my hands, and as I was soaping up, I glanced at the test, still sitting there on the vanity—and I saw the pink line. It was faint, but it was there. I was not a fool after all. I was pregnant.

Embryonic Life as a Central Concern

Before this point, many readers probably expected me to address questions around embryos: When does life begin? Is it ethical to create, manipulate, and destroy embryos in the lab? For those who identify as pro-life, the sanctity of embryonic life—an embryo's status as a human being—is the central reason that they oppose abortion, reproductive technologies that involve manipulating or destroying embryos, and contraceptives that prevent implantation of fertilized eggs. So why leave such a vital concern until now, near the end of the book?

After reading myriad perspectives, I've concluded that making one's view of embryonic life the central concern in reproductive ethics is potentially misleading and overly simplistic, even for those who have a strong, well-reasoned pro-life ethic. I have learned that those who are pro-life can (and do) support the use of reproductive technology under some circumstances, and that those who are pro-choice, for whom the status of embryos is not a central concern, can (and do) oppose certain uses of reproductive technology. In this chapter I will not spend much time on traditional questions about embryos, such as when life begins, and will explain why I don't think those questions are the most important ones to be asking. Rather, this chapter will focus on the limits of traditional pro-life and pro-choice arguments, as well as on the complex and emotionally charged ways that aspiring parents and others perceive, imagine, consider, and talk about human embryos.

Pro-Life Tunnel Vision

In 2010 the evangelical magazine *Christianity Today* asked me to write five hundred words on what should be done about the thousands of frozen embryos left over from IVF procedures. My answer in a nutshell: I don't know. But I do know, from my own experience and study data, that most people who undergo IVF don't really think about such questions until they have to—and then they struggle because the questions are so complex and emotional, and they are unprepared and alone. My article suggests that the best way to address the problem of leftover embryos is to provide better resources for prospective parents to participate in ethical, emotional, and theological reflection so that they are better equipped to make decisions.

My piece was published alongside two others. Ron Stoddart of Nightlight Christian Adoptions argued that making frozen embryos available for other infertile couples to adopt is the only ethical choice for those who believe life begins at conception. Bioethicist David Cook focused, as I did, more on process than remedy, arguing that everyone with a stake in fertility treatment—including clinics, parents, and governments—needs to take responsibility for embryos created through IVF. Cook's piece, however, included a line that left me cold: "For those who believe in the sanctity of life, adoption, donation, or *the development of artificial wombs to carry children who are not adopted* seem the morally acceptable options for preserving life" (emphasis added). To be fair, five hundred words is a terribly constraining article length, especially for a topic as fraught as reproductive ethics. If he had been allowed more words to work with, perhaps Cook would have conceded that artificial wombs raise significant ethical questions of their own—questions around identity, children as commodities, and artificial wombs affecting adoption.

A 2010 study revealed that adult children who were conceived through anonymous sperm donation, aware that they were conceived via technology in a fee-for-service endeavor, carry more uncertainty about their identity than either adopted or biological children. The study reminds us that family connections, including biological and genetic ones, are core components of human identity. Uncertainty about such connections can lead to feelings of loss, alienation, and anxiety. Many adoptive parents and their children, even those in loving and happy families, cope with loss and grief as part of the adoption process. For children gestated and birthed from artificial wombs, questions around biology, genetics, and family would certainly be significant and, without proper attention being given to them, potentially damaging.

In the dystopian novel *Brave New World*, babies are created and gestated by artificial wombs, genetically programmed and educated to fulfill predetermined roles that ensure the efficient functioning of a consumer society. This is fiction, we know, but in a technological and consumer-oriented society such as ours, it is easy to imagine that babies created in labs and birthed by machines would likewise be treated as products, subject to quality control and designed to meet the demands of consumers—parents and the wider culture that defines what good parents do. As I discussed in chapter 3, even well-meaning parents who balk at the idea of "designer babies" face cultural pressures to maximize their children's chances for success. It is really not a stretch to imagine prospective parents going through portfolios of embryos available for adoption, scrutinizing the biological parents' profiles, and choosing those with the potential to be attractive, healthy, and smart, to be popped into an artificial womb and gestated on their behalf.

Artificial wombs, I suspect, would appeal to the same impulses that lead prospective parents to handpick donor eggs, donor sperm, and gestational surrogates to conceive and bear children genetically and biologically unrelated to their intended parents, instead of adopting already-born children. Parents could choose embryos based on their biological parents' genetic attributes and then completely control their baby's gestational environment, without getting involved in the complex interpersonal and biological issues raised by surrogacy. Artificial wombs might become the first choice even for some fertile couples motivated to do everything possible to ensure their babies' health. Pregnant mothers can control their diets, medications, prenatal care, and physical fitness, but they can't do as much about environmental toxins or their own susceptibility to illness or injury. Some women just don't like being pregnant. Some women have severe nausea, premature contractions requiring bed rest, or other significant complications and discomforts. Artificial wombs would allow couples to proactively avoid pregnancy-related stress and risks. Although many fertile women would never choose to forgo pregnancy, in a culture that so values choice, control, and health, some certainly would.

Would access to controlled technological reproduction via artificial wombs prevent some infertile couples from adopting children who are already born and awaiting a home? Would widespread use of artificial wombs lead to the conception and birth of children without parents waiting to take them home, thus adding to the number of orphans? Both scenarios seem possible.

The ethical and cultural implications of using artificial wombs to gestate parentless embryos are huge. Yet an educated, thoughtful bioethicist casually mentioned artificial wombs as a "morally acceptable" response to what he perceives as the central concern in reproductive ethics: giving every human embryo a chance for life. Treating embryos with dignity is certainly a vital concern. But making the protection and preservation of embryos the sole concern can lead to tunnel vision that blinds us to other important ethical issues, as well as theological ones.

Again using the example of artificial wombs, although adoptive families illustrate that a biological connection between parents and children is not absolutely necessary, Christians also embrace the connection between our physical bodies and our spiritual lives. The Bible is full of characters for whom physical experiences—childbearing, infertility, sexual encounters, illness, cooking, eating—were central moments in their spiritual journeys. Jesus was no ethereal spirit, but a flesh-and-blood man who ate and drank, wept and slept, bled and died. The physical bond between mother and child during gestation and birth is not merely a technical process, but rather a physically, spiritually, and emotionally transformative one. Tossing that process out and replacing it with machines—in the name of preserving embryos—is not only morally questionable but also spiritually shortsighted.

Tunnel vision is also apparent in much literature and discussion about reproductive ethics among conservative Christians. William Cutrer, MD, and Sandra Glahn, a Christian educator, have coauthored several books on infertility for an evangelical audience. Their 2010 book *When Empty Arms Become a Heavy Burden* includes several chapters on the ethics of assisted reproduction. The authors reduce moral deliberation to procedural thoroughness, giving the impression that couples need only to think through technical issues, such as cost, the risks of twin and triplet pregnancies, steps to take to avoid having leftover frozen embryos, and the legal status of children conceived with third-party help, such as gamete donors and surrogates. The book gives the impression that—because the authors perceive the treatment of embryos as the central moral question raised by reproductive technology, and because they do a good job of discussing ways to avoid having many leftover embryos (such as limiting the number of eggs that are fertilized in IVF)—they see other moral questions as unimportant, failing to address some significant issues altogether. If *When Empty Arms Become a Heavy Burden* is the only book that a couple reads while undergoing fertility treatment, they are going to have an insufficient perspective on the ethical questions raised by the treatments they are considering—a perspective limited by the authors' equating the ethics of reproductive technology with the preservation of embryonic life.

As I have blogged extensively on reproductive ethics, I've also noticed that many pro-life comments on articles online betray a similarly limited perspective. Some bloggers and commenters condemn all reproductive technology because it manipulates and destroys embryos; others perceive techniques such as IVF as pro-life because they literally create new lives. But in both cases, even Christians who have given reproductive ethics some thought seem unaware that reproductive technology raises significant moral issues beyond how we treat embryos.

Pro-Choice Tunnel Vision

Tunnel vision, as with most human failings, is not exclusive to particular groups or ideologies. Liberals have a moral tunnel vision of their own when it comes to reproductive ethics, focusing primarily on choice and women's rights.

In her 2007 book on assisted reproduction, *Everything Conceivable*, journalist Liza Mundy describes the difficult place that Planned Parenthood finds itself in as reproductive technology becomes more sophisticated and ubiquitous. The organization's leaders are forced to address "whether every choice made possible by science is a choice pro-choicers should welcome into the broad philosophical tent of choice." Focusing primarily on choice and rights makes responding to new reproductive technologies tricky. Pro-choice advocates, for example, tend to perceive parental rights as paramount. But if parents' rights always trump children's rights, that leaves little room for concern with how children conceived via gamete donation or surrogacy will incorporate their genetically and biologically complicated beginnings into a healthy sense of identity. A strict focus on parental rights means that parental well-being (e.g., their joy at having the children they long for) is always more important than children's well-being (e.g., their potential confusion or sense of loss upon learning that they are biologically and genetically connected to adults other than the parents they live with).

Likewise, if reproductive freedom and the right to choose are the central concerns of reproductive ethics, then how do we respond when doctors and fertility patients use that freedom to make choices that many people, liberal and conservative, find troubling, such as sex selection or genetic screening for nondisease traits? Mundy writes that "reproductive liberty can be, and is, invoked by fertility doctors who want to justify performing every new lucrative procedure, no matter how untested."

Because the pro-choice movement centers on women's rights, sex-selection technology poses a particularly thorny problem. Sex selection to ensure male offspring stems from ancient patriarchal notions that boys are more valuable than girls. American fertility doctors treat patients from Asian, Middle Eastern, and African cultures who take advantage of our unregulated fertility industry to use PGD to ensure that they have baby boys. In some cases the mothers-to-be proactively seek the treatment, and in others they appear to be under pressure from husbands and extended families to deliver much-desired male children. Some U.S. fertility clinics even proactively market PGD for sex selection to people of Indian and Chinese descent by advertising in foreign-language newspapers and partnering with overseas fertility clinics that provide the first steps in treatment, before sending their patients to America for egg retrieval and embryo transfer. In such cases, accessing fertility treatment may be less about a woman's freely exercising her choice than about her obligation to conform to ancient cultural and familial practices that are fundamentally oppressive to women.

Here in the United States, sex selection is used more often to ensure girls than boys. Many mothers in particular feel that their family is not complete until they have the daughter they have always dreamed of. Even this preference for girls, however, may ultimately undermine women's interests by reinforcing entrenched definitions of femininity that focus on physical appearance. Mundy noticed that "in the sex-selection chat rooms I looked at, there were lots of women looking forward to dressing little girls in pink outfits and putting pretty bows in their hair."

Mundy discussed the sex-selection dilemma with a Planned Parenthood spokeswoman who, while concerned about sex-selection technology, said she did not think it should be banned. "Her fear," writes Mundy, "is that any effort to direct any reproductive decision made by any individual is to call into question all decisions made by all individuals, including, of course, the decision to abort." Mundy, on the other hand, argues that "it should be possible to (1) accept a woman's moral right to choose whether or not to continue an unintended or unwanted pregnancy and (2) reject an infertility patient's right to infinitely select desired traits in offspring." But that will only be possible if those on the left are willing to question or reframe their rhetoric of choice and parental rights and to recognize that unlimited choice can be as problematic as no choice at all.

When *Does* Life Begin?

While an exclusive focus on preserving embryonic life may lead to troublesome tunnel vision, treating embryos with dignity is clearly important for Christians. The psalmist, for example, praises God by saying, "You created my inmost being; you knit me together in my mother's womb. I praise you because I am fearfully and wonderfully made" (Psalm 139:13–14 NIV). The idea that God has known and loved us always, from the moment we were conceived, can be tremendously comforting. We have an obligation, then, to explore how God the Creator's intimate knowledge of every person in the womb influences how we perceive and treat embryos.

During my ongoing e-mail correspondence with our theologian friend Chris about our PGD decisions, I initially ignored the traditional question "When does life begin?" Daniel and I had attended a talk at our church given by a local professor of ethics and had been convinced by many of the arguments he made against seeing an embryo as a fully realized human being. The speaker explained that a fertilized egg cannot be seen as a particular, individual human being until after the time that twinning can occur and basic physical systems, such as nerves and circulation, begin to form (around fourteen days after conception). Until that point the fertilized egg is potentially several human beings, not one in particular. While there are a variety of perspectives on embryos among the major theistic religions, many religious thinkers have similarly argued that an embryo cannot be considered an individual with a soul until a certain number of days after conception (the number of days differs among traditions). One Jewish argument holds that an embryo cannot be considered a human being until it implants in a mother's womb.

These arguments made sense to me. Efforts to name embryos as full human beings seem to ignore some fundamental truths of pregnancy and birth. Human technology has not yet found a way for even the healthiest fertilized eggs to become babies without a woman's womb. I wonder if this is not merely biological fact but also a hint that our human identity is rooted in relationship, that defining a "human being" requires acknowledging that we are not simply bunches of cells cobbled together into a functioning organism. We can, literally, not become human without an early and fundamental connection to another person (yet another reason why artificial wombs would have significant ramifications for human identity and culture).

Insistence on viewing embryos as complete people also ignores the fact that, while pro-life groups continue to press so-called personhood initiatives for embryos, most of us do not treat embryos as full-fledged people in other contexts. Choice USA made a humorous video in response to the personhood initiative on Colorado's ballot in 2010. In the video, a pregnant woman is charged for an extra movie ticket and forced to play doubles at the tennis courts because her fetus counts as a separate person. When women miscarry, we not only don't publish death notices and hold memorial services; we often don't even acknowledge the loss. That lack of acknowledgment is painful for couples who experience miscarriage, and our culture could do a better job of honoring the relationship that parents-to-be have with their unborn children. It's odd, however, that the uncertainty about embryo identity apparent in how we respond to miscarriages flies out the window when we start talking about abortion rights or reproductive technology. Women who miscarry are expected to pick up and carry on as if nothing of great value was lost, while pro-life advocates argue that abortion is equal to murder.

When I was grappling with decisions about PGD, I was not predisposed to spend much time in pondering the status of embryos. Chris, however, encouraged me to reconsider that predisposition. He did not engage in arguments about when life begins. Instead he argued that the question of when life begins—when an embryo or fetus can be considered a full-fledged human being—was not really the right question to ask:

Obviously none of us know the answer to this question [of when an embryo is fully human] in any scientifically provable way. That uncertainty is significant, but I don't think the question is meant to be seen as a scientific issue. . . . In my heart of hearts, I am suspicious of any debate about the question "When does an embryo/fetus become a human being?" . . . The embryo question . . . really asks, "Where can we draw a boundary that allows us to manipulate whatever this fertilized egg might be with a clean conscience? How can we relieve ourselves of the sense [that] we might be offending a dignity that deserves our respect?" Those are valid questions, but they aren't neutral questions. . . . What makes a human being matter ethically, what gives us dignity, is not some quality (such as individual differentiation or rationality/ autonomy). It is rather that God loves us and calls us by name. . . . To put too much weight on that question (is a 13-day-old fetus nonhuman in a way that a 15-day-old one is human) is an impulse toward human self-sufficiency, which is not the impulse we need to nurture if we want to learn the skill of living in God's grace. Our task in life—to really absorb that God loves us, wants to be in relation with us, and to live in a way which is open to that—is something we can do whether our kids are healthy or sick, whether we know confidently or are agnostic about the status of thirteen-day-old embryos.

In other words, science provides an insufficient framework for examining the moral status of embryos. Approached from a scientific perspective, the question of whether a fertilized egg is a human being can be answered in different ways, depending on the information we have and how we interpret it. Though I'm still sympathetic to arguments, such as those offered by our church speaker, against defining embryos as fully realized human beings, I've also concluded that how we *define* embryos is less important than how we *approach* them.

When does life begin? We can't really know from a scientific perspective. But we can pay attention to whether we are treating embryos as clumps of cells to do with as we will or as potential vessels for persons to inhabit, as beloved creatures of God. Science and our modern medical and parenting cultures tend to approach embryos empirically, as bits of flesh whose worth is determined by our scientific understanding of their particular traits at particular times. Our faith requires that we approach embryos reverently, as gifts whose worth is determined by the nature of the God who gives them.

Natural versus Technological Selection of Embryos

If God knows and loves us from our conception, if parents deeply mourn the loss of even an early pregnancy, then we cannot in good conscience treat embryos as mere clumps of cells. But we also must acknowledge that in natural reproduction, embryos are lost all the time, often before we've had any chance to consider them at all. Embryos fail to implant; they implant and develop into something called a hydatidiform mole, which is essentially a useless bunch of cells; they die in the womb for reasons known and unknown.

This truth of God's creation is not an excuse for unlimited human intervention in embryonic development, any more than the fact that God's creation relies on predator-prey relationships is an excuse for humans to exercise unlimited predatory behavior over other species. The frequency of natural embryo loss, often for no clear reason, can be a lesson in humility, reminding us that procreation is not merely a technical process that humans can master; it is the mystery through which God bestows the gift of life. Anglican bioethicist Oliver O'Donovan argues that nature's randomness is linked to God's providence:

> The element of chance is one of the factors which most distinguish the act of begetting from the act of technique. In allowing something to randomness, we confess that, though we might, from a purely technical point of view, direct events, it is beyond our competence to direct them well. We commit ourselves to divine providence because we have reached the point at which we know we must stop making, and simply be. . . . Randomness is the inscrutable face which providence turns to us when we cannot trace its ways or guess its purpose. To accept the fact is to accept that we cannot plan for the best as God plans for the best, and that we cannot read his plans before the day he declares them. . . . We do not, in natural begetting, bring sperm and ovum together, and as it were, forcibly introduce them to each other.

But it's important also not to assume that because embryo selection occurs naturally, it should *only* occur naturally. In Liza Mundy's words, we need to avoid the temptation to "fetishize nature" by rejecting any human involvement in reproduction and assuming that we're messing with a natural system that works perfectly, because it often doesn't.

The Liminal Nature of Embryos

Politically charged pro-life/pro-choice debates have made it difficult to contemplate embryonic life because these debates insist on absolutes. Either embryos are the same as babies, or they are merely bunches of cells subject to their parents' choices. I think most people, when pressed, would say that neither is quite true. Embryos occupy an in-between place. They are liminal; they serve as a doorway or threshold between one state of being (individual sperm and eggs that only have the potential for life until they join with the other) and another (the definitive, transforming presence of a newborn child). The threshold is essential for connecting those two states of being; it cannot be lightly discarded any more than a house can be built without doors. But it's also more a passage to something vital than a destination in itself.

The liminal nature of embryos and the importance of naming and considering their in-between nature more fully are apparent in two phenomena: Cultural responses to miscarriage and parents' perception of their unborn children, whether they are embryos in a laboratory freezer or images on an ultrasound screen.

In her memoir *Waiting for Daisy*, Peggy Orenstein details her experience with infertility and several miscarriages, describing the liminal nature of embryos and miscarriage this way: "What I'd experienced had not been a full life, nor was it a full death, but it was a real loss." On a trip to Japan shortly after one miscarriage, she realized that other cultures are not as unwilling or unable to name the loss of embryonic life as our culture is, observing that "there is no word in English for a miscarried or aborted fetus. How better to bury a topic than to make it quite literally unspeakable?" Japanese people, in contrast, have a word for miscarried or aborted fetuses—*mizuko*, "which is usually translated to 'water child.' Historically, Japanese Buddhists believed that existence flowed into being slowly, like liquid. . . . A *mizuko* lay somewhere along the continuum, in that liminal space between life and death but belonging to neither."

Orenstein took advantage of a semipublic Japanese ritual called *mizuko kuyo*, in which mothers grieving the loss of miscarriage or abortion leave trinkets (caps, flowers, baby toys) on small statues of infants placed in Buddhist temples. *Mizuko kuyo* is a ritual of apology (to the unborn child who did not have a chance at life) and remembrance. Orenstein left her trinkets and said her good-byes. She left the temple while still grieving but grateful for the ritual that allowed her to name her loss. Even Christians who reject the specific Buddhist beliefs that inform *mizuko kuyo* might learn something from Japanese culture's willingness to recognize and name the liminal nature of embryonic life.

Taking part in *mizuko kuyo* revealed to Orenstein the insufficiency of American pro-life/pro-choice rhetoric to capture the complicated relationship between parents-to-be and their unborn children. As a pro-choice advocate, Orenstein believes that "social personhood may be distinct from biological and legal personhood," but admitted that

> the zing of connection between me and my embryo felt startlingly real, and at direct odds with everything I believe about when life begins. Nor have those beliefs—a complicated calculus of science, politics and ethics—changed. I tell myself that this wasn't a person. It wasn't a child. At the same time, I can't deny that it was something. How can I mourn what I don't believe existed? The debate over abortion has become so polarized that exploring such contradictions feels too risky. In the political discussion, there has been no vocabulary of nuance.

The *New York Times* editor Bill Keller experienced a similar disconnect between his pro-choice rhetoric and his experience as a father when his son was prenatally diagnosed with significant abnormalities:

> The technology that informs you [that] your future baby is mysteriously endangered also makes him real, a boy-like creature swimming in utero. . . . Yes, I know how shamelessly the anti-abortion lobby has exploited this illusion to give tadpole-sized fetuses the

poster appeal of full-grown infants. But no amount of reasoning about the status of this creature can quite counteract the portrait that begins to form in your heart, with the poetry of the first heartbeats.

Through their family's losses, these authors recognize that our debates over abortion, embryos, and reproductive technology are sorely lacking in recognition of the hard-to-pin-down, emotional realities of conception, pregnancy, pregnancy loss, and birth.

One might think that parents would find it easier to define their relationship with IVF-conceived embryos that never made it out of their Petri dishes, rather than embryos that were the subject of excited phone calls announcing a pregnancy or fetuses whose tiny toes were visible on ultrasound. But studies show that even with embryos left over from IVF cycles, parents struggle with reconciling practical concerns with their emotional responses.

Ambivalent Conceptions: How Parents Perceive Embryos

A 2005 study found that 72 percent of couples interviewed who had gone through IVF treatment had not made and were not in the process of making decisions about what to do with their leftover embryos. That study cites an earlier report revealing that more than 80 percent of couples who had planned to donate their embryos for research or to other couples changed their minds. In the 2005 study, "several couples commented that contemplating the fate of their embryos was harder than their decision to go forward with the donor oocyte [and IVF] procedure itself."

The study found that "the factor that contributes most significantly to the difficulty of the disposition decision is the complex nature of the couples' conceptualization of their embryos." Couples saw their embryos in a variety of ways: as biological material, as living entities, and as "virtual children," whose interests must be considered. Some were uncomfortable with donating to another couple because they would lose control over their genetically related children, for whom they felt responsible. Some couples "incorporated [the embryos] into their family structure by referring to them as siblings of their living children. This view complicated the consideration of donating embryos as it gave rise to concerns about the possibility of their living child inadvertently meeting and starting a relationship with a child conceived from a donated embryo." Couples saw embryos as a "genetic or psychological insurance policy and considered the possibility that their embryos might provide some medical benefit to their living children at some future time" or might be "potential replacements for their living children should they be lost through illness or accident." Embryos also became "symbols of the infertility that had dominated their lives for so many years." Some wanted to use their embryos up to have more children, and for some, the unused embryos fed an ongoing desire for more children even when that was impractical.

Parents' complex relationships with their embryos, whether they exist in laboratories or the womb, defy simplistic pro-life/pro-choice arguments that define embryos either as equal to fully developed children or as mere biological matter.

Judging the Whole on the Basis of One Part

One of the most troubling moral aspects of using PGD to decide which embryos get a chance at life is that at the embryonic stage, we can know and interpret only tiny, discrete bits of what will become a multifaceted human life. When Daniel and I decided to transfer the single embryo that tested negative for OI and destroy three embryos that tested positive, I was aware that we were destroying embryos that could become children like Leah. At the time, three-year-old Leah was talkative, bright, and endlessly curious, with a sweet pixie face and a head of gorgeous, bright blond curls to boot. She has grown into a top-notch student, an avid pianist, and a science and animal lover who plans to be a veterinarian. Leah has the enviable ability to be at home in her own skin; she knows who she is, what she likes and doesn't, and is not the type of kid who does something just because her friends are doing it. She has struggled with having OI; a new fracture inevitably leads to some mild depression and fierce anger at having to cancel plans or be singled out at school. But OI is only a part of who she is, and she is remarkable. We destroyed three embryos because they carried the genetic mutation that Leah and I carry. What remarkable traits might those children have had? No genetic test can predict the fullness of a human life.

When Amy Julia Becker's daughter Penny was born with Down syndrome, she and her husband were initially angry because prenatal testing had indicated that the chances of their baby's having Down syndrome were very low. But their fears and anger dissipated as they began loving Penny as a whole, flesh-and-blood child rather than a diagnosis. Becker writes:

> A prenatal diagnosis of Down syndrome couldn't have given me what I wanted. A diagnosis gives the words "mental retardation." It gives numbers and statistics. It gives a list of potential medical problems. But Penny's life is more than a list of medical concerns. No prenatal test could have told me that my daughter would love to sing but have trouble carrying a tune. Or that she would have a pitcher's aim when throwing a ball but lack the coordination to play tennis. Or that she would love the color pink but show no interest in dressing up like a princess. When Penny was first born, I was afraid that her disabilities would make her less than human. Instead, her disabilities have exposed our common humanity.

When we select out embryos with specific genetic mutations, we are judging an embryo's fitness for life based on one trait, without knowing anything about what other traits the resulting person might have. If we use that fact as an absolute argument against technological embryo selection, however, we fall into the same trap of judging people's worth based on their traits. Suppose we argue that selecting out an embryo carrying an OI mutation might rob humanity of a free-thinking, intelligent, science-loving future vet like Leah. Such an argument implies that free-thinking, intelligent, science-loving vets are valuable *because* of their free-thinking, intelligent, science-loving ways—that these positive traits outweigh the pain and disability of OI. In that case we're still judging embryos based on purely human calculations of worth based on intelligence, abilities, and contributions to society.

But at the very least, we need to acknowledge that when we select for and against embryos based on discrete genetic traits, without considering the complex wholeness of every human being (a wholeness

impossible to see at the embryonic stage), we are inserting our preferences, based on our very limited knowledge, into the normally ran-
dom process of procreation—a randomness in which we might, like
bioethicist O'Donovan, see the hand of God.

Rejecting Disabilities or People with Disabilities?

When people decide whether or not a child should be gestated and
born based on whether or not that child has a genetic disorder, are
we asserting that people with genetic disorders do not have worth?
In other words, does rejecting embryos with particular disabilities
imply a rejection of people with the same disability?

When Daniel and I used PGD, we did so because we rejected the
disability in question, not *people with that disability*. Trying to conceive a child without OI did not mean that I did not value myself or
that we did not value our daughter.

Doctor Janet Malek, a medical ethicist at East Carolina University, wrote a paper on this topic, published in the April 2010 issue
of the *Journal of Medical Ethics*. Malek argues against the idea that
individuals' use of reproductive genetic technologies, including
PGD and prenatal diagnosis, implies a devaluing of people with disabilities. She concludes that "the choice to avoid creating a life with
disability may reflect a negative view of the disability itself, but not
of persons who have it." Malek comes to this conclusion by discussing a series of thought experiments. For example, if you were about
to cross a street and a guardian angel told you that a driver was going
to run the red light, strike you, and cause you to become a paraplegic,
does your decision to avoid disability by not crossing the street imply
that you do not value paraplegics? Most people would recognize that
a desire to avoid serious physical injury (or to protect one's child
from serious physical injury) arises from innate impulses toward
self-preservation and care, not discriminatory attitudes toward those
with serious physical injuries.

Malek acknowledges that there may be other ethical considerations with reproductive technologies. But she rejects the argument
that use of such technologies implies an unacceptable devaluing of
people with disabilities. Again, this conclusion makes sense to me,

given our situation of having two well-loved family members with OI but wanting to spare additional children the same diagnosis.

Embracing Questions instead of Answers

The 2005 study by Nachtigall and others (cited earlier), examining parents' perspectives on their leftover IVF embryos, also found that couples were unprepared to make decisions about their embryos because they were more focused on getting pregnant than on the decisions that might follow. This focus, combined with a medical culture centered on achieving pregnancies, means that considering the moral dimensions of fertility medicine is usually not part of the plan, for either patients or clinicians. Our clinic had a psychologist available to discuss ethical and emotional concerns, but we were never encouraged, much less required, to meet with her. While Christian friends offered support, we found church resources inadequate.

In America today, discussions about reproductive ethics tend to take place on op-ed pages, in political campaigns, and in blog-comment sections, where readers post knee-jerk reactions to articles in which writers share their difficult reproductive decisions. Such discussions tend to feature unequivocal answers to questions about when life begins, how we treat embryos, and what parents want—answers that are then lobbed into opposing camps. But for those who are actually in the midst of making difficult reproductive decisions, we provide few resources and little space for them to consider the questions whose answers are seldom clear.

When Daniel and I were going through PGD, we made the best decisions we could with the resources we had. I do not regret going through PGD, and though I've thought more seriously about the embryos we had destroyed in the years since our PGD cycle than we did at the time, I don't regret that decision either. But I wonder if our decisions and experience would have been easier if both our fertility clinic and our church had been equipped and available to raise good questions and help us consider answers. The market-oriented clinic culture may be entrenched, but clinics could quite easily have a psychologist, social worker, or other counselor take substantial time at IVF information sessions to educate patients about the emotionally charged and morally weighted questions they will face, encouraging them to proactively meet with counselors or their own religious advisers. Such encouragement would not necessarily have helped me come to clear conclusions about our embryos and whether destroying the ones we didn't use was right. Even now, after eight years of contemplating reproductive technology, I find questions around embryos to be more elusive than ever. But at least an invitation to seek guidance would have acknowledged that decisions about embryos, babies, pregnancy, and parenting carry moral and emotional weight that deserves our attention.

Questions to Think About

1. Do you consider yourself to be pro-life or pro-choice? How do your religious beliefs inform that position? How does your pro-life or pro-choice perspective inform your approach to reproductive technologies such as IVF and PGD?
2. What beliefs, facts, and experiences inform how you think about human embryos and whether particular human interventions in embryonic development (abortion, genetic screening, research on embryos, and so forth) are or are not ethical?
3. Does genetic screening of embryos for particular disorders/ disabilities imply a devaluing of people with those disorders/ disabilities?
4. What resources or changes in practice might better inform and help people who are making difficult reproductive decisions?

6

Where We Ended Up

Family Portrait: October 3, 2003

In the weeks before our second baby's birth, we spent entirely too much time at the downtown hospital complex. In early September, I was briefly hospitalized on the labor and delivery (L&D) ward for kidney stones. The following week we were back on the L&D floor for a parents-to-be hospital tour; later the same day we took Leah to the children's hospital ER because she was complaining of pain in her hip and couldn't walk. They diagnosed a possible hairline fracture at the top end of her femur—a fracture that could not really be treated, so they sent us home. Two weeks later, on September 29, Leah landed in the ER again, this time with the unmistakable fracture to her left forearm that I described in the introduction.

That fracture happened on a Monday evening. On Wednesday, I had a sudden surge of energy. As my pregnancy approached its end, I had completely lost interest in cooking—a favorite domestic hobby—but on this day, I flung open the latest *Bon Appétit* and pulled together a chicken-and-squash chowder. That done, I turned to a basket of apples we had picked the previous weekend and made an apple crisp. Aware that this sudden domestic efficiency was possibly a prelabor nesting urge, I stayed up late, paying the month's bills. Secure in the knowledge that the lights would stay on and my family would not starve if I were to have a baby in the coming days, I went to bed but slept fitfully. By the following evening, I was clearly in labor, though the baby's due date was still two weeks away. Leaving

Leah in my mother's care, Daniel and I went out into the night air, chilled by the first frost of the season, to drive to the hospital.

The most excruciating point of my textbook labor was a botched epidural, in which the needle went into a blood vessel and so had to be redone, all while I was having hard contractions three minutes apart. The anesthesiologist later admitted she had been nervous about messing with a fragile spine. I wish she had said so when she first arrived: I could have told her that an epidural needle was not going to break my back.

Not long after the epidural was finally in and working, a resident showed up and snapped on her latex gloves to check my progress. She felt around for a while, then said to our nurse, "Can you get an ultrasound machine? It feels like she's only a fingertip dilated, but I know she was at five centimeters a couple of hours ago. I'm not sure what I'm feeling." I noticed that her glove was streaked with blood and a dark sticky goo that was clearly baby poop. I knew, as she did, that what she was feeling was not my cervix, but my baby's bottom. As she hooked up the ultrasound machine, she said quietly, "I always check a baby's position when I admit a woman in labor." She seemed to be trying extremely hard to be professional and not yell, "Why didn't your doctor check the baby's position?" That was exactly what I was wondering.

The ultrasound confirmed what we already knew: the baby was breech. The resident said, "You know what that means, don't you?" to which I answered, with only a small sigh of disappointment, "Yup, I sure do." Leah had been delivered via planned C-section because she was breech, and I had prayed, thought, and agonized about the decision to try a VBAC (vaginal birth after cesarean). I had pored over medical journal articles on VBAC that Daniel brought home from the library where he worked. I had discussed the pros and cons with several of the doctors in my ob-gyn group and with an obstetrician in California who had worked with many women who had OI. I knew, without a doubt, that my crooked little body was capable of pushing this baby out. But at the moment when I learned the baby was breech, I didn't care anymore. Knowing that the baby was breech and I was clearly nearing the end of my labor, I was afraid she was going to come out before they had a chance to cut her out, and

I didn't want to go through a vaginal breech delivery. The certainty and passivity of the operating room sounded like heaven.

The hospital staff seemed to be moving too slowly, getting things ready as though I was just having a wisdom tooth removed, rather than surgically delivering a breech baby who was making it clear she was ready to be born. After what seemed like hours of preparation (but was really less than an hour), my doctor finally tugged the baby free and handed her off to a nurse. The room was quiet. I could not see the baby, but I knew she was in a far corner, under a warmer, tended by several nurses. Months later Daniel confessed that he was terrified at this point: the baby looked blue and lifeless. It was probably only thirty seconds of silence, but it seemed a very long time. Finally we heard a staccato burst, more like a chirp than a cry. But it was enough. As my doctor prodded around in my belly, cleaning and closing me up, he said gently, "Look over to your right, Ellen. There's your baby." And there she was. Five-pound, eight-ounce Margaret Ellen Dollar. Our baby Meg.

Once Meg was weighed and warmed, they swaddled her into a tight bundle and let Daniel hold her while my incision was closed. We were all sent off to the recovery room, where I held her, with the soothing heat of a warming light shining on both of us. I didn't care one bit that this birth had not gone according to plan. She was here. And I knew for sure that she did not have OI.

In contrast, when Leah was born four years earlier, we didn't know yet whether she had OI. Daniel, who accompanied Leah immediately after birth to have a piece of her cord biopsied for OI testing, told me upon his return to my bedside that Leah's eyes were a "funny" color. Knowing that blue sclerae—whites of the eyes—are one sign of OI, I slammed a heavy door shut in my head, refusing to let in even the suspicion that she might have OI. But I noticed the eye color too, and how soft and loose her shoulder joints seemed. I worried that an unknowing nurse would pick her up by her ankles or arm and break something. That first six weeks of Leah's life were peppered with moments of excruciating anxiety. We had no clear diagnosis on paper, but our suspicions that she had OI grew with every comment on her bluish eye color; with our noticing how floppy she felt every time we picked her up, unlike most newborns, who curl themselves into tidy little bundles; and with every comment from someone that her long, skinny fingers and toes looked just like mine.

When I was pregnant with Meg, I accepted that she too might have OI, but I was unwilling to go through that sickening lurch of uncertainty every time I looked at my newborn, every time someone else wanted to pick her up. I wanted to know before she was born whether or not she had OI, and I wanted to know for sure, based on genetic testing, not merely on ultrasound images of her bones.

One criticism leveled at reproductive technologies such as high-resolution ultrasounds, prenatal diagnosis, and genetic testing is that in satisfying parents' urge to know as much as possible about their children's gender, appearance, and health before birth, these technologies take away the mystery and grace of accepting a new life exactly as it comes, without any preconceived notions. In writing about reproductive ethics, I have interviewed many parents and prospective parents about their childbearing decisions. One interviewee asked this thought-provoking question: "Shouldn't we always be prepared to welcome the difference and potential difficulty of a child? There are so many mysteries to a child, even a genetically 'normal' child, that we could never know. Would we like to know if she will die of leukemia at six? Or be an alcoholic by thirty? Do we want to know if she'll be crippled in a car accident? My sense is that it would radically change reproductive technology if we resisted the urge to know and lived in the painful but hopeful potential of the present."

While receiving children without condition is vital, so too is knowledge that helps parents and doctors manage birth and a child's first weeks of life. I have discovered during my interviews that many parents like me—those who have had a child with a genetic disorder—see prenatal diagnostic tools as important sources of information. For example, Amy Julia Becker, whose work I have cited several times and whose oldest child has Down syndrome, wanted information to help plan for the births of her second and third babies. She and her husband refused amniocentesis because it carries a small risk of miscarriage, saying they honestly did not worry about whether or not the babies would have Down syndrome. They already knew firsthand that a child with Down syndrome is as much a gift as any other child. But knowing that they were at higher risk of having another child with Down syndrome and that serious heart defects can sometimes accompany that syndrome, they agreed to noninvasive tests such as regular ultrasounds. They wanted to know about serious problems that might threaten their child's life or require specialized medical attention immediately after birth. Prenatal testing can allow for planning and provide some peace of mind for parents; it does not necessarily indicate a need to predict the future or a refusal to fully accept our children as they are.

Because prenatal genetic testing was the only foolproof way to know before birth if Meg inherited OI, I had an amniocentesis done in May 2003, at sixteen weeks' gestation. On an early June evening, Leah and I returned from a dinner at church and found Daniel sitting at home with a secret, a surprise he couldn't wait to unwrap for us. The genetic counselor had called to let us know that the baby did *not* have OI. The next night, Leah was walking across the living room floor and her lower leg just folded beneath her, for no good reason. She had a displaced fracture of the fibula and tibia—both lower leg bones.

So once again, a watershed moment in our parenting journey was accompanied by one of Leah's fractures. I wasn't sure whether to thank God for the positive amnio results or not. I couldn't believe that God had orchestrated this baby to be free of OI, because that would mean he hadn't done the same for Leah. But I did feel grateful, relieved, and free to welcome our new baby when she arrived without holding my breath every time someone else picked her up, afraid of hearing a sudden shriek, indicating that my newborn had just broken a bone.

Reflections on Being Undone

As I left the hospital with Meg when she was three days old, I had an irrational urge to bolt from my nurse escort and run to the opposite end of the maternity floor. The postpartum-nursery section of the floor and the labor-delivery section were parallel to each other, separated by a corridor of vending machines and elevators. As I emerged from the postpartum area, blinking and fuzzy from three days of narcotics-induced dozing, I saw the doors to the L&D area for the first time since the night I had gone into labor. No one is allowed behind those doors unless they are a laboring woman or one of the three support people, designated in writing, that each woman is allowed. But for a moment I considered whether I could sneak in behind a nurse coming back from her lunch break, just to see it one more time.

I had an obsessive need to revisit every detail of Meg's birth because it, like every birth, was unique and life changing. But also because I had been rather sure, before Meg arrived, that I was done. Done. There would be no more babies. That seemed like the clear, responsible choice, the choice we *should* make, given the fifty-fifty chance that any baby we have will inherit a chronic, disabling condition, and that we had spent nearly two years consumed by agonizing decisions about whether and how we should have this baby. So this was my last chance to see the place where I gave birth to my last baby after my last pregnancy. Thinking of it that way made me so sad. Right there in the hospital corridor, before Meg had even breathed a particle of outside air, I began to wonder if I was really, really done.

That first wisp of longing, coming as it did on the heels of major surgery, lack of sleep, and my stunned examination of this new life—how could I have forgotten how *tiny* their bottoms are?—was surely going to be temporary. It would curl up and out of my stretched and stitched and bleeding body, hover around my weary and love-addled brain, and disappear into the air. After I was shocked back to life by a hungry baby, who demanded that she be either fed or held every minute, and by a busy four-year-old, who talked nonstop from the moment she got out of bed (usually no later than 6:00 a.m.)—I would remember all the reasons why I should not have another baby, and that would be that. . . .

Except that, when we took Meg for her one-week checkup, our pediatrician told us that he and his wife were expecting their third baby. Their older kids were nine and eleven years old; back when the children were little, he told us, they had thought about a third, and it just seemed so overwhelming. Recently they had been wishing they'd had a third. Then they realized they could still have a third, and so they did. This is exactly what I did not want to hear. I had wondered if couples ever, years later, regretted their decision to be done with childbearing. Here was proof that, yes, sometimes they did.

After all the anguish and struggle over my genetic baggage, OI was no longer a frightening-enough threat to rule out a third baby. That struggle had shown me that our family has much raw material with which to craft a life; most of it is sound, strong stuff that helps us carry the weight of this disability.

On top of that, after Meg's birth, Leah entered a time of physical progress in which OI faded into the background. The broken arm just before Meg was born ended the fracture cycle she had been in. At first we counted her fracture-free time in months and then in years. From ages four to nine, Leah had only one fracture—an uncomplicated broken wrist. We can't say why. It was probably a combination of good medicine (a few months before Meg was born, Leah began taking medication to increase her bone density) and good luck (the longer she went being active and without a fracture, the stronger her bones became, making them less likely to break). All along we knew that OI is a capricious disorder, and Leah's good years came to a crashing end when she had a scooter accident at age nine, which left her with several broken bones requiring surgery. But for those few good years, OI was more like a distant cousin whom we heard from occasionally and less like an intimate member of our nuclear family. And as Meg grew from infant to toddler, we learned how it felt to have an active, resilient child who could fall off the couch without more than a bumped head. The possibility of having a third child who might have OI began to seem less scary and immediate.

But there were still other, more mundane reasons that I thought I should be done with having babies. My common-sensical brain was crowded with worries that seemed silly and unimportant next to our genetic risks but that nevertheless preoccupied me for much of Meg's first year. For example, our house was very small. When Meg was a baby, I sat in the middle of the night, nursing her and mentally rearranging the furniture in her room until the bridge of my nose ached. Would it be possible to fit two children and their stuff into this little room? It would be a little crowded, but yes, perhaps it could work.

I worried too about the fact that neither of our cars had space for three child safety seats; we would need a minivan, or at least something with a wider back seat. But we had scant savings and little wiggle room in our monthly budget for another car payment.

Nevertheless, the daytime equivalent of my nighttime furniture rearranging was a new fascination with the back seats of cars. I would make a point of parking next to some model of wagon or van or SUV that I'd never examined before; then I'd try to take a good look at the back seat without appearing too suspicious. If no one was around, I'd take a closer look at the cargo area too. Besides three kids and their seats, we'd need room for multiple strollers and possibly Leah's wheelchair, which she used when she had a leg fracture and couldn't walk.

All this looking and measuring was exhausting. Really, I told myself, it would just be easier to forget the third-child idea. More than anything, I wanted to stop thinking about it anymore, to just know which it was to be: was I done or was I undone? Daniel was refreshingly clearheaded about the whole thing. He had always wanted a big family. He knew that, given my age and OI, three was going to be our limit, and that's what he wanted. But I couldn't figure out what *I* wanted. I waited for a gut feeling that never came. I was searching for clarity, using a logical process of weights and measures, scrutinizing rooms and car seats, calculating how many more years of good mobility I might have, adding up how much money per month we would have to save to buy a bigger house or pay for three college educations.

Then one Sunday at church, I heard a sermon on the Scripture passage in which Jesus says that whoever loses his life will find it (Matt. 10:39). For the first time in my life, I listened to this passage without developing a sudden keen interest in my fingernails or the lovely scarf draped over the woman's shoulders in front of me. This passage always made me feel guilty; I was so certain that I was not following it. Sure, I chaired the church outreach committee, and my pre-kids career was doing communications work for several worthy service organizations. But these efforts did not come close to the radical selflessness Jesus was talking about. I always figured that to follow these words, I had to do *exactly* as Jesus had done—hang out with society's outcasts and be essentially homeless and prepared to die.

But this time, when I heard that passage, it got under my skin and shimmied its way into my brain, where it hung out amid all my third-child angst. Then it wrapped itself around the hard edges of my overcalculated anxieties and wore them away. For the first time, I saw that motherhood offered me a way of living this lost/found paradox.

I know that many women have lost themselves in trying to make their husbands and children happy and have gained nothing much worthwhile in return. I am lucky to have a husband who understands that motherhood and housewifery cannot fill my every need, who graciously shoos me out the door for my book-club meetings, lap swimming, or dinner with friends. Yet I still sometimes feel as though motherhood has made me into a nobody, has robbed me of everything that once made me interesting. After years of being home with my children, I'm still surprised when Daniel asks me what I did today, and though I barely sat down from breakfast to supper, I can't think of a single interesting thing to tell him.

Back in my Potter's House Church days in D.C., we often talked of the difficulty of being called to a "small work," a work that is not impressive or spectacular by the world's measurement. Motherhood is the ultimate small work. Yes, it is huge too. But it is full of smallness—the tedium of fixing the same cream-cheese sandwich on whole wheat every day for a child's lunch and picking up dozens of Legos off the floor every evening, or the ridiculously overblown anticipation of a pediatrician's appointment because it provides an opportunity to get out of the house and talk to another adult.

But when I look beyond the smallness of daily life with children, I can see how I am being forced to lose the self that craves control and quiet and grown-up words, how I am finding a different self. The former self rarely gets what it wants and is often crabby about it. The new self realizes, once in a while at least, that motherhood, in taking away the things I crave, has forced me to be more welcoming of life in all the forms it comes to me, no matter how messy, inconvenient, boring, or threatening. It has forced me to spend less time in thinking about what I want and more time in seeing what I have. It has made me more hospitable.

What I want is a house like you see in catalogs, with sunlight streaming through a smudge-free window to splash on a sparkling hardwood floor, with nary a crushed Cheerio or tiny plastic animal in sight. What I have is a home where each of us feels welcomed to do those things that make us say, "I had a good day." The kids' art table, rather than being a tidy and labeled oasis like those in the Pottery Barn catalog, is home to haphazard piles of markers, paper, and interesting found objects (a deflated balloon, Christmas tinsel). Our garden will not win any awards for landscape design, but it is frequently abuzz with butterflies, bumblebees, and dirty-footed children. Most of the time the grass is a little too long, the bathroom sinks are filmed with old toothpaste, and we rotate through the same dinner menus that are not nutritionally complete. But there is freedom for me to write, for Daniel to go for a Sunday afternoon hike, and for the kids to roam the cul-de-sac with their neighborhood friends.

What I want is to write fine books that sell in the tens of thousands and earn us enough for Daniel to pursue his dream of being a man of leisure, while I preside over my catalog-ready house and pay someone else to clean it. What I have are small bits of prose, written during snatched moments and better than anything I wrote during my ten-year career in nonprofit communications because motherhood has sharpened my voice and focused my passions.

What I want is an ache-free, beautifully wrought body, smooth and balanced like a piece of well-made furniture. What I have is a crooked, creaky, and well-used body, which looks as though it were pieced together out of spare parts. Today the consequence of offering my body to my children—as their incubator, transporter, comforter— is sore knees at bedtime. Later, who knows what the consequences will be—more fractures? a wheelchair? I will certainly pay a price in lameness for having offered this body to my children; but in bearing and rearing children, my body has done exactly what I wanted and needed it to do, for the first time in my life.

Ultimately the reflections on faith and reproductive technology that consumed the months leading up to Meg's conception had the most influence on my thoughts about a third child. Through that process, I became convinced that life is a gift, always a gift, no matter in what form it comes, no matter what pains or struggles it will know. Our culture offers us medical technology as a way to make life predictable and safe. It also tells us that responsible parents shouldn't have more babies unless they can provide them with all the things necessary for a twenty-first-century American life: a room of their own, an SUV with side air bags and third-row seating, a fully funded investment account for college. All these things tempt me. I want the certainty and comfort and safety they offer.

But I am called to be a mother to the children I have now, not in some future time when I can better afford them or when gene therapy offers a cure for OI. My small work is to choose gratitude and grace in the face of the chaos and uncertainty that will be part of human life as long as the work that God began at creation is ongoing, as long as God's kingdom is not yet fully here. Most of the time I am called to be grateful and gracious amid the small chaos of motherhood: The kitchen floor, mopped just this morning, is by afternoon covered with crusty noodles and blobs of yogurt. The little one who learned to sleep through the night long ago is waking in the wee hours because of an ear infection or scary dreams. I spend twenty minutes wrestling the children into their snow gear, and after five minutes outside, they are ready to come back inside for lunch and hot cocoa.

And then Leah slips on the kitchen floor and lands hard, hands slapping loudly against the vinyl, and I hear that familiar choking cry of pain. Her hands are red and raw from playing in the snow, so the slap against the floor is especially painful. This time we escape without anything breaking. But I'm reminded again that my daughter, today so bright and whole and straight, will one day again be crumpled and broken. And then I turn on the television after the tsunamis in South Asia and see a man cradling his dead child, a boy about Leah's size, and I'm reminded that even strong and healthy children can be swept away when an audacious ocean jumps its borders. In the face of all that, my small work is to remember and to teach my children that God made us and God loves us, so there is nothing to fear.

I knew that if we had a third baby, I would lose more of myself to the small chaos of motherhood. There would be more crumbs and smudges, more sharp and cruel retorts uttered after I have lost all patience, more trips to the emergency room for fractures (Leah's? mine? the new baby's?). I would trip over the baby's bouncy seat because we had no more unused corners where it could sit out of the way, and spend Christmas morning wondering where the heck we're going to put all this crap. I would drive a clunky used minivan, probably beige. I would lie awake imagining what we would do if I broke an arm or leg and couldn't care for my kids, and then I would stop imagining, because there is no scenario that is less than terrifying.

I finally decided that, after two children, I was not done. I was undone, in every sense of that word. My undoing—the very real and painful losses of control that come with motherhood—was necessary for me to grow into the person (the mother, the writer) God made me to be. On January 27, 2006, I gave birth to a baby boy named Ben. Somehow, we beat the fifty-fifty odds. Ben does not have OI.

A well-meaning friend at our church looked me in the eye once and said about Meg and Ben not having OI, "Don't you see? God wanted you to trust him with your children. He made sure it would be OK." I don't know about that. In one of his e-mails, Chris said that God never calls us to more than we can bear. I don't know about that either. It seems to me that lots of us are living with burdens that we can't bear. I can't bear the memory of Leah with her femur snapped and swollen, screaming and choking in pain. I can't bear knowing that my body harbors an enemy that threatens to steal away my ability to care for my children, who are young enough that they need not only my love and my listening and my voice reading them a bedtime story, but also my flesh and my muscle and my bone.

My default response when people express relief and joy that my two younger children escaped my OI gene is to say it's just luck. Not good luck, mind you. Saying it is good luck seems to be a betrayal of Leah. Just luck. Just the way things turned out. But sometimes I don't know about that either. When we conceived Meg and Ben, we did it recklessly, but also faithfully, believing that God would help us whatever the outcome. It is impossible to know for certain in what form that help came, in what form it continues to come. Neither Meg nor Ben has OI, and that makes it possible for me to care for all three of my children essentially on my own for most hours of most days. So I thank God for that simple fact—for their strong bones—even if I'm suspicious of the idea that God is responsible for them.

A Broken Body Redeemed

I do believe God has called me to have my three babies, though I'm still not sure why. Maybe it has to do with how motherhood is changing me, forcing me to choose faith over fear, risk over security, the chaos of a fully lived life over the calm of a safely lived one.

Certainly having three children requires a surrender of self that having two children only hinted at. Every moment is given to meeting someone's need. Even when the need is mine—to sit down for a sandwich or read a novel for my book group—I meet it with urgency, knowing that a child's need will certainly interrupt me sooner than I would like.

Maybe this giving of myself to others' needs is the "why" of my vocation as a mother. I don't know. But I do know this: I have felt betrayed by my body because of what it can't do and what it isn't. Yet in bearing children, my broken body has done a powerful thing. It has given life to three brand-new people. A new ability to see my body as capable and worthy, beautiful and powerful, is one of the surprise gifts of motherhood.

When Ben was six months old, we traveled to Omaha for an OI Foundation conference. As we were checking in at the hotel, I glanced up and saw a young woman. She was less than five feet tall, with a square and thick torso over thin legs, and shoulder-length brown hair. She was pushing a baby stroller that came up too high on her, to her chest, making her look even smaller. I stared for just a moment, not long enough for her to notice, taking her in. I had never seen another mother who looked just like me. As I looked at her, all the strain I didn't even know I was carrying around, all the self-consciousness of being a tiny, crooked, fragile mom in a world of tall, straight, strong moms—it all fell away. Here was a mom who looked just like me. And she was beautiful, capable, and strong. Which meant I must be beautiful, capable, and strong too—as strong as those moms who effortlessly dangle an infant seat on one arm while balancing a toddler on the opposite hip—because lifting and carrying and bending over to bathe my children are acts of will and courage as much as they are acts of strength.

I am beginning to pay the price for giving my body to my children. My pregnancy with Ben wore me out physically in a way my first two pregnancies did not. I tore cartilage in my knee when I was eight months pregnant. When Ben was delivered by C-section, my epidural did not work completely, so the birth was a drug-fogged blur of activity punctuated by pain. Since Ben's birth, I have had two arthroscopic surgeries on my knee, am living with chronic pain, and use strong pain medication regularly for the first time in my life.

Many days I feel inadequate, ashamed, and just plain sorry that I can't do all the things my children need me to do. I couldn't walk and bounce a fussy baby around the house to soothe him. I can't carry a tired child for the last twenty-five yards to the car.

And yet I also feel more proud of my body since Ben's birth. The first time we took him and the girls to the beach, I was walking along the boardwalk, clad only in sandals and a bathing suit, as Meg ran ahead of me to the restroom. I noticed people glancing sidelong at my scars, my limp. To my surprise, I felt no embarrassment or shame. I looked ahead to Meg, her strong little legs clomp-clomping against the boardwalk as she ran. I thought of the other two children back with Daniel at our beach blanket. There was Leah, golden-curled and lanky, her long limbs crusted with sparkling sand. And there was Ben, fat and scrumptious, napping in his car seat. This fragile, broken body gave life to all of them. That, to me, is redemption.

7

"The Only Way Is Hard"

A Christian Approach to Reproductive Technology

*T*here is no moral to my story. This is not a fable ending with a quotable object lesson. Daniel and I eventually abandoned our PGD attempt for emotional, financial, and ethical reasons. But I will not frame our story as one in which we eventually saw the error of our ways and came to understand IVF and PGD as unacceptable for Christians. I am grateful that Daniel and I were free to make our reproductive choices with conscience and faith as our guides, without having to also negotiate laws governing those choices. But I will not frame our story as being essentially about the need to protect reproductive freedom.

Rather, the most important lesson I have learned from conceiving, bearing, and raising three children, given the fact of my debilitating genetic disorder, is the same lesson that Wendell Berry offers in his poem "The Way of Pain":

> For parents, the only way
> is hard. We who give life
> give pain. There is no help.
> Yet we who give pain
> give love; by pain we learn
> the extremity of love.

It's hard to cope with infertility or the harsh realities of genetic disease. It's hard to go through emotionally, physically, financially, and morally strenuous procedures such as IVF and PGD. It's hard to forgo those procedures and the control (or illusion of control) over our procreation that they offer. It's hard to have a baby, and it's hard not to have a baby. It's hard to finally understand that no matter how we become parents—through natural conception, technological reproduction, or adoption—we can never clear the pain of life out of our children's paths.

Our great solace in all these hard endeavors is the reality of love— the love we have for our children, the love they have for us, and the love that God has for the whole lot of us. Wanting, bearing, and raising children are hard. But we hold up; we even thrive in the midst of parenthood's struggles and heartbreak only because of love and its many corollaries—grace, forgiveness, redemption, hope.

So I'm not going to conclude with a pronouncement about whether or not reproductive technology is morally acceptable, or offer a step-by-step guide for Christians who are contemplating whether to use IVF, PGD, or other technologies to have a baby. Rather, I will offer some broader suggestions for how parents, medical personnel, pastors, and others who support those grappling with complex reproductive decisions can approach the difficult, controversial ethical questions raised by ever-expanding reproductive technologies.

Stories Matter

This book centers on my story not just because it might prove helpful to those in similar situations (though I hope it does) but also because hearing and contemplating people's real-life stories is essential for pondering sticky ethical questions. There is a name for moral deliberation that gives significant weight to particular people's stories: narrative ethics. Traditional ethics uses a juridical process, in which experts consider the various moral questions raised by a particular situation, explore those questions by using established ethical principles, and render a judgment based on which principles they see as most applicable. Narrative ethics is less cut-and-dried because it allows room even for amateurs to weigh and discuss the complexities of a particular person's story, acknowledging that such factors as the person's intentions and past experience are relevant to their current situation. Narrative ethics strives less for a clear-cut decision about which choice is morally superior, and more for consensus on which choice seems best in the context of people's stories.

There are inherent problems with such an approach: It is difficult to come up with a decisive answer about what is right, and those wrestling with an ethical question can be swayed by their personal feelings about the people involved. For example, in the essay collection *Stories Matter: The Role of Narrative in Medical Ethics*, two authors describe a bioethics class discussion about a couple who conceived quadruplets via IVF and, after testing all the embryos for Down syndrome, did selective reductions of the embryos (none of which had Down syndrome) so they could have one boy and one girl. After one student blurted out that the parents would next ask for a "blond-haired, blue-eyed yuppie with a date book attached," the class discussion changed significantly:

> The students had a moral characterization of the participants in the narrative, [and] they also had a story line. . . . The interesting, cautionary aspect is that they had an extremely difficult time returning to a more objective or balanced reading of the story. They understood that the comment had unfairly transformed the couple into perpetuators of Nazi eugenics experimentation, but their entry into that story line made it hard for them to imagine the couple as two deeply loving human beings, willing to devote everything in their lives to caring for the children they hoped to bring into the world, an equally plausible characterization that would move narrative, reader, and the interpretive community into a significantly different relationship with the case and the people involved with it.

In another case study, an ethics committee discussed the case of a sixty-year-old woman who wanted to conceive a child via donor-egg IVF with her much younger second husband. Committee members conceded that their ultimate decision to allow the patient to undergo IVF was influenced by their favorable reaction to the patient's demeanor and story. She was poised, attractive, and articulate. Her extended family supported her decision. Her own father had a child at age sixty-five with a much younger wife. She was physically fit, and there seemed to be no medical reason why she could not safely bear a child. Would the committee have reacted so favorably to a different sixty-year-old woman whose story and attitude were not so appealing? Possibly not.

Narrative ethics requires that we eventually decide which story line we will believe. We have to decide which story is paramount: the one about parents who will only welcome a particular kind of child and will do anything, including pushing back against normal biological limitations, to satisfy their parental desires, or the one about loving couples using technology to fulfill the understandable and oh-so-human desire to create a family.

Deciding which story to believe requires an informed community of listeners who help the parents uncover their motives and assumptions. Narrative ethics is more about deliberate, informed, and supportive conversation than the dispensing of authoritative opinion. As two of the *Stories Matter* authors explain, "It is in the dialogue, and there alone, that we experience the rhythms of asking and answering, speaking and listening, feeling and thinking, giving and receiving that lie at the center of the work we do, not the *either/or* but the *and/also* of compassionate moral deliberation and ethical decision-making."

The church is (or should be) the ideal place for parents-to-be to grapple with difficult reproductive decisions in the company of supportive, compassionate people who share their faith and values. But it is frequently not such a place. Pastors, fellow church members, and prospective parents themselves often lack comprehensive information about reproductive technologies and the ethical questions they raise. Their opinions and conversations are often informed by sensationalist, superficial media accounts (about the "Octomom" or the latest celebrity to have twins via surrogate, for example) or worn pro-choice/pro-life arguments that are not always relevant. The medical clinics where prospective parents go to explore technological reproduction are focused on helping patients achieve pregnancy as quickly and cost-effectively as possible; thus they likewise are ill-equipped to provide a supportive space in which aspiring parents can share their stories and talk openly with people who will support and inform their search for moral guidance.

But I am hopeful that the lack of supportive communities where parents can contend with their reproductive decisions is a problem that can be remedied. I am confident that aspiring parents—along with their friends, family, pastors, counselors, and medical providers—can become better informed about reproductive ethics and better equipped to engage in sensitive, meaningful conversations that will empower parents to make sound ethical decisions. I've developed five guidelines for how those involved in such conversations can help create and participate in supportive communities for reproductive decision making:

1. Acknowledge the moral dimension of reproductive decisions.
2. Make space and take time for moral deliberation.
3. Remember that stories matter, but stories are not *all* that matter.
4. Balance private decisions and public consequences.
5. Watch your language.

Acknowledge the Moral Dimension of Reproductive Decisions

We live in a highly technological society where sophisticated medical techniques, equipment, and interventions are commonplace (e.g., CT scans, MRIs, robotic surgery, pacemakers, manufactured replacement joints). It is tempting to lump reproductive technology in with other medical breakthroughs, presenting them as value-neutral technical achievements that address medical problems (infertility, genetic disorders) and don't require serious ethical consideration. And indeed, IVF and PGD *are* technical achievements able to relieve the concrete suffering that people experience as a result of infertility and genetic disease.

But reproductive technology does not merely address medical problems. Those with no medical problems can and do use IVF, PGD, gamete donation, and surrogacy to have children for other reasons—such as being in a same-sex partnership, intending to become a single parent, or wanting to voluntarily postpone childbearing for financial or lifestyle reasons. Furthermore, even when reproductive technology is medically indicated for infertility or a genetic disorder, it substantially alters the dynamics that have governed human life, culture, and relationships for all of human history.

Children conceived via technology can have relationships with three or more parents, each of whom contributed something to the child's conception and upbringing—genetic material, gestation and birth, day-to-day care. Parents can guarantee that they have a son or daughter or ensure that children don't inherit particular genetic traits, including traits that many people would not consider problematic enough to justify genetic screening. A grandmother can bear her own grandchild, as occurred in February 2011 when a sixty-one-year-old woman gave birth via C-section to her own grandson, conceived via IVF with her daughter's egg and son-in-law's sperm. PGD doesn't cure genetic disorders; its successful use merely ensures that children with particular genetic disorders are not born, which is a significantly different endeavor.

Furthermore, the market-oriented nature of fertility medicine, along with a lack of regulation and insurance coverage, can potentially exacerbate social injustices. For example, parents with plenty of money to pay for PGD can more easily avoid having children with costly and debilitating genetic disorders than their less-well-off counterparts. Fertility medicine advances come out of the clinic instead of the lab, raising questions about the ethics of human experimentation. Whether fertility treatments pose long-term health risks to mothers or babies remains an open question. Studies looking at health risks to women who take fertility drugs for their own treatment or to serve as egg donors are especially rare.

Whatever our opinion on particular uses or outcomes of reproductive medicine, can we at least agree that such fundamental shifts in how children are conceived and born deserve deliberate contemplation? Medical practitioners often come across as willfully disengaged from the ethical implications of their work. In 2010 an American fertility clinic raffled off an IVF cycle with a donated egg in a marketing effort aimed at British women who travel to the United States to access our larger pool of donor eggs. When media reports sparked objections to the raffle, clinic personnel insisted they were simply offering a medical service to a needy clientele. The response came across as disingenuous: Did clinicians really not recognize that raffling human tissue (a donated egg) in response to market dynamics that make the tissue more available in one country than another raises some ethical concerns? The news media also often fails to adequately engage ethical concerns. The media's normalization of reproductive technology was especially apparent, for example, in the coverage of Robert Edwards's Nobel Prize, which I discussed in the introduction.

The frequency and quality of conversations around reproductive ethics would significantly improve if everyone involved—parents, clinicians, genetic counselors, clergy, government regulators, and journalists—would simply acknowledge that reproductive technology is changing how we perceive human life, reproduction, health, and family relationships. We may disagree about the technology's precise moral implications and its true potential to radically change life as we know it, but perhaps we can start by agreeing that the implications are worth talking about.

Make Space and Take Time for Moral Deliberation

As Protestant bioethicist Gilbert Meilaender has observed, "[Reproductive] technology carries its own momentum which, if not irresistible, is nevertheless very powerful." A common theme in memoirs of infertility is that, once you step into a fertility clinic, you essentially step onto a treadmill and find it very hard to step off. As treatment progresses without success, clinicians offer ever more sophisticated and expensive treatments to help patients achieve pregnancy. In our experience, there was very little encouragement for us to take time to think about what we were getting into (beyond the logistics of how to give myself an injection, for example), and little understanding of our desire to step back periodically to consider whether or not to proceed. Recall, for example, how our clinic's financial staff person was utterly perplexed at the idea that we wanted to figure out how to pay for our IVF/PGD cycle before committing to start the cycle. Remember also the study cited in chapter 5 revealing that fertility clinic patients generally don't think much about what they will do with any leftover IVF-conceived embryos; they and their caregivers are completely focused on achieving pregnancy, not on what might come afterward.

Clearly, clinics exist to provide treatment, not ethical counsel. It seems reasonable, however, for clinics to use introductory information sessions to encourage patients to consider the emotional, spiritual, and ethical questions they may face during treatment. Furthermore, clinics can encourage patients to access professional help for engaging those questions, either from an in-house counselor or an outside mental health professional, spiritual adviser, or clergyperson. Our clinic, despite having a psychologist on staff, did not proactively encourage us to call on her or anyone else to address emotional, spiritual, and ethical concerns. I have talked to other fertility patients since then, however, who say their clinics did raise key issues early on, including questions about how they wanted to handle leftover embryos. Perhaps this aspect of fertility treatment is improving, or perhaps it depends largely on where people are treated. In any case, frank acknowledgment that patients will contend with difficult questions and may want help in answering them should be as routine a part of fertility treatment as the lessons on how to self-administer medications.

Also in our experience, our pastors and Christian friends were largely ill-equipped to help us engage moral questions, not because they didn't care, but because they were unfamiliar with current technology and its ethical implications. Research by the progressive Religious Institute indicates that our experience was not unusual. In their resource *A Time to Be Born: A Faith-Based Guide to Assisted Reproductive Technology*, the Institute calls on religious leaders to more effectively support congregants coping with reproductive decisions by educating themselves about current technology and related ethical questions; addressing reproductive ethics from the pulpit, in congregational study groups, with other religious leaders, and from a public-policy standpoint; and providing compassionate, knowledgeable pastoral care for church members coping with infertility, adopting a child, or otherwise dealing with reproductive concerns.

Clinicians, clergy, and other professionals could do a better job of thoughtfully addressing ethical questions with aspiring parents; yet parents themselves can also strive to make time and space for moral considerations. It's not an easy thing to do, particularly amid the physical and emotional stress of undergoing fertility treatment while also carrying the burdens of grief and anxiety that often accompany difficult childbearing decisions. It is impossible to completely think through every scenario and every ethical nuance of every possible decision ahead of time. But it's important to take some time—before visiting the clinic or genetic counselor for the first time if possible, and even in the midst of decision making and treatment—to discuss decisions with a partner, friend, family member, clergyperson, counselor, or other trusted confidant. I encourage people to read the stories of others who have faced similar situations; there are many excellent memoirs and blogs available, some of which I have listed in the bibliography.

I also urge people to tell their own story, again and again if necessary, to people they trust to receive it graciously. The ongoing e-mail conversation I had with my friend Chris when Daniel and I were making our decisions gave me an opportunity to tell my story, confess my fears and hopes, and consider perspectives that were different from mine. My storytelling and the conversation it inspired were valuable tools in our decision making. I encourage all those facing hard reproductive decisions to seek out a similarly safe space in which to tell their stories. Doing so will bring some clarity to what can be a very murky process.

Remember That stories Matter, but Stories Are Not *All* That Matter

Sharing, hearing, and accepting the stories of how people are making reproductive decisions is central. But are people's stories the sole, exclusive tool we should rely on for making ethical decisions? In a word, no.

The problem with focusing solely on our and others' stories is that we humans are prone to self-absorption, self-pity, and a tunnel vision that puts our own pain, problems, and desire for happiness front and center. We are all too capable of justifying poor decisions and bending or obscuring the truth to suit our needs. In short, and to put it in Christian terms, we are all sinful and overly caught up in the self.

Giving weight to individuals' stories in reproductive decision making forces us to embrace and wrestle with complexity and nuance; most people's stories do not naturally divide into clear categories of black and white, right and wrong. But if we focus exclusively on people's stories, if we give complete moral authority to an individual's interpretations of a particular situation, then we risk moral relativism. Any decision, no matter how troubling, can be justified if we are unwilling to challenge an individual's perspective (or unwilling to allow others to challenge ours). We must be willing to look beyond our own and others' stories, invite other perspectives to inform our own, and apply time-tested moral principles to our situation. For Christians, these principles include such basics as the worth of every human being; the surprising and transforming power of limitations, weakness, self-giving service, and humility; the possibility that suffering can be redemptive; and the centrality of self-giving love.

Earlier in this chapter I mentioned a case in which a sixty-year-old woman wanted to use assisted reproduction to bear a child with her much younger second husband. Her story was compelling—she was attractive, healthy, and eloquent about her and her husband's desire for a child. The ethics committee who heard her case ultimately decided to approve her IVF treatment. Her story convinced them to honor her unusual request. Later on, however, the medical practice that performed the woman's IVF set an age limit for patients wishing to use assisted reproduction and asked her doctor not to perform a procedure like this again. While the ethics committee gave primary weight to the patient's story, her doctors gave more weight to other concerns and decided that helping postmenopausal women have babies was ethically troubling, no matter how compelling a particular woman's story. Does the potential for parental happiness justify the significant medical risks involved in IVF, even for a healthy woman? What about the ethical questions around egg-donor risks and compensation, given that postmenopausal pregnancy requires donated eggs? Relatively few postmenopausal women have gone through IVF; might there be significant age-related risks that we don't fully understand yet? Are value and meaning to be found in accepting one's biological limits rather than striving to overcome them? What obligation does an older mother have to her child, knowing that she will likely be facing health declines associated with aging when her child is still relatively young? Concerns with postmenopausal childbearing could potentially trump even the most appealing story.

When we share and hear our own and others' stories, we also need to be aware of cultural tendencies that can give both human suffering and human happiness more significance than they deserve. Ours is a highly individualistic culture, which puts great value on people's self-expression and self-definition. We tend to inflate the significance of both our suffering and our need for happiness, leading people to feel that they have a right to pursue any means necessary to lessen their pain (no matter how commonplace) and maximize their happiness.

For example, years ago I saw a television news segment on parents who signed their children up for a controversial drug trial involving injections of human growth hormone. The parents of one boy, who was healthy but smaller than average, decided to enroll their son in the trial despite the potential for unknown side effects because, in their eyes, their son's suffering justified extreme measures. How did he suffer? He felt inferior to his taller brother. He could not always compete with peers in sports where height provides an advantage. Feeling inferior to his brother and his peers often led the boy to tears. The boys' tears and his parents' compassion for his suffering were genuine. But is it really appropriate to use risky medical interventions to assuage suffering that arises from the simple fact that all of us have limits? None of us can do everything well. All of us fail in endeavors that our siblings, friends, and peers succeed in. Part of embracing the gift of life is learning to live within one's limitations, even when they are painful, and seeking the best ways to exercise our unique gifts, not searching for a technological salve for every wound.

Balance Private Decisions and Public Consequences

With reproductive technology, the act of procreation, which normally takes place behind closed doors and between two people, becomes a public and technologized process involving dozens of experts and eliciting advice from professionals, family, friends, and even strangers. Fertility patients are well aware (I certainly was) that their decisions, motives, and actions are scrutinized in a way they wouldn't be if they conceived the old-fashioned way. And frankly, that's not fair.

But fair or not, private childbearing decisions have public consequences. As bioethicist Jacob M. Appel has written, "Parenting is among the most personal choices anyone ever makes. At the same time, no other individual decision has as significant a societal impact. Finding a careful balance between personal autonomy and the public welfare is often a considerable challenge."

Thousands of individual stories and childbearing decisions can contribute to significant cultural change. The postwar baby boom is a prime example. The baby boom, the high birthrate in America in 1946–64, was the result of thousands of couples deciding to have babies. They might have talked through those decisions at length, in hushed conversations at the kitchen table, or conceived their babies impulsively or accidentally. However they did it, considering the cultural change they might usher in wasn't part of the process. These were purely private, intimate decisions. But usher in cultural change they did: their children, by sheer force of numbers, went on to influence how Americans view sex, politics, health, aging, money . . . nearly everything.

All childbearing decisions are influenced by external factors. The boomers' parents were influenced by postwar phenomena such as the G.I. bill, economic stability, and increasing suburbanization. Today's parents are influenced by unprecedented choice and available technology, as well as a widespread ethos of parental control and responsibility. Likewise, childbearing decisions—not individual decisions so much as the collective power of many individual decisions—influence the culture in which they occur. As I've discussed in this book, decisions about whether, when, and how to use reproductive technology could influence and even radically change how we value and treat people with disabilities, our expectations for how parents can ensure their children's ultimate health and success, the number of parents that children interact with (or don't) as they grow up, adoption practices, the government's role in reproductive choice and freedom, and more.

But infertile couples and those living with genetic disease usually don't make reproductive decisions in the public square, weighing their effects on culture and society. They make them in the intimate, fragile confines of the human heart. I'm convinced that ethical questions about reproductive and genetic technology will only really be heard, and will only spur real change, when we speak to people at that level, where people care not only about having babies but also about the babies they will have. Childbearing decisions are some of the most personal, intimate decisions people make. Ultimately it's the parents who live, day after day, with the consequences of those decisions—with the grief of living without much-wanted children or with the medical, financial, and emotional struggles of raising a child with a genetic disorder. At the same time, parents need to be aware of the larger cultural dynamics their decisions might influence. This is a difficult but vital balance to recognize, between private and public, personal and cultural.

Watch Your Language

This suggestion is most relevant for theologians and academic ethicists whose language often alienates people (or simply fails to engage them). Theological and academic language can be inaccessible to people unfamiliar with a discipline's jargon; in some cases, professional theologians and ethicists use words that don't reflect people's lived experiences.

The Roman Catholic Church has traditionally offered the most comprehensive and consistent Christian position on reproductive technology. The official Catholic view is that no reproductive technology—from contraception and artificial insemination to IVF, PGD, and surrogacy—is acceptable. I admire the Catholic position for its integrity and thoroughness, but I struggle with its substance, largely because it doesn't adequately recognize the unique circumstances that individual couples face when making childbearing decisions (it fails to incorporate and speak directly to people's stories, in other words). Official Catholic documents tend to address reproductive decisions by using language that fails to acknowledge the emotional realities of wanting and having children.

For example, two major Vatican documents addressing reproductive technology, the 1987 *Donum Vitae* and 2008 *Dignitas Personae*, repeatedly refer to artificial fertilization techniques, including IVF and ICSI (in which single sperm are injected directly into an egg) as intrinsically "illicit." Use of such a loaded, negative word virtually ensures that readers who have used or considered IVF will feel defensive and accused of something shockingly corrupt. "Illicit" is an appropriate label for the latest sex scandal involving a politician and his expensive escort, not for a loving couple seeking relief from the pain of being unable to bear children. (Although, to be fair to theologians, readers can also interpret theological language inaccurately. In her memoir *The Early Birds*, author Jenny Minton claims that Catholic bishops consider her IVF-conceived twins "undignified." While Catholic documents name the protection of human dignity as a motivation for rejecting reproductive technology, they do not label IVF-conceived children as "undignified" in the way that people tend to use that word, meaning unseemly or ill-mannered.)

The U.S. Catholic Bishops' 2009 statement opposing assisted reproduction, *Life-Giving Love in an Age of Technology*, is quite readable, but many of the bishops' word choices are difficult to swallow. In one passage objecting to donor gametes and surrogacy, the bishops' document states, "In an important sense, the spouses [who rely on gamete donors or surrogates] have decided not to be fully the mother and father of their child, because they have delegated part of their role to others." I recently had a friend over with her ten-month-old daughter, who was conceived via IVF using a donor egg. As her daughter keenly followed her mother's every move and protested the minute she left her sight, my friend said, "I challenge anybody to tell me I am not this child's mother." The bishops' language is off-putting and even offensive to parents who know from emotionally rich and valid experience that using donor gametes is not a decision to "delegate" the role of mother and father to others.

Several parents to whom I've talked likewise object to the Catholic argument that use of donor gametes and surrogacy "violates" their marriage by bringing third parties into a process designed by God to only involve two people. "Violate" is another harsh and loaded word, associated with deplorable and illegal acts; criminals violate the law, rapists violate women. It also fails to speak to the actual experience of couples who have children by using donor sperm, donor eggs, or surrogates, many of whom find that their marriage is stronger at the end of their reproductive journey than it was at the beginning. Involving third parties in reproduction raises valid ethical concerns, including the question of whether it interferes with God's plan for marriage as being a union between one man and one woman, from which children may arise. But the word "violate" alienates many readers for whom such a word is far too grim to describe their experience of going through assisted reproduction with their spouse.

As Christians, we know that experience is not *all* that matters. We know that theological and spiritual truths transcend experience even as they are rooted in it. On Sunday mornings, my experience is that I'm eating a tasteless wafer dipped in sweet wine, while my theological understanding tells me that I'm taking into myself the body and blood of my risen Savior. Truth is more than just experience.

But experience (that is, our stories) must count for something. Theological discourse that fails to incorporate experience falls short. Communion is meaningful in part because it speaks to us in a language we understand not just with our brains but also with our bodies and our hearts—the language of hunger and thirst, of need and fulfillment, of wounds and healing.

Theological arguments that ring false because they don't acknowledge the tangible realities of human experience are too easily discarded. The idea that mothers and fathers are delegating their parental roles when they use donor gametes appears ridiculous when you witness a donor-conceived baby who clearly knows exactly who her mother is.

When we talk about reproductive technology, we're talking about having and loving babies, some of the most physically, emotionally, and spiritually transformative experiences of human life. Few other life experiences lay so bare our bodily limits, capabilities, and needs, plus our emotional vulnerability and the centrality of familial love. Our language must reflect those realities.

The Stories We Live By

Were my husband and I right or wrong to pursue PGD? Were we right or wrong to abandon it? The short answer is that I don't know. Our story is simply our story. Living that story, I broadened my understanding of disability, limitation, choice, suffering, and the legacies we leave our children, but I've been unable to reach a firm conclusion concerning whether reproductive technologies such as IVF and PGD are acceptable for Christians under some circumstances, and not under others. That's why I won't end this book by telling readers what to do, but rather by encouraging them to tackle important ethical questions with diligence, compassion, and wisdom.

An acquaintance whose daughter also has OI was once confronted by a brazen stranger who asked, "What's wrong with her?" The mother's response was "Nothing. Normal is just a setting on the washing machine." It was a great answer, a true answer. Nothing is wrong, in a fundamental sense of our human identity as children of God, with those who have OI or other genetic disorders.

But something *is* wrong with our bodies. They are not as they were designed to be. While I do not advocate fixing what's wrong at all costs—there are compelling, important reasons why Christians should tread carefully when considering IVF and PGD—I do think there are plenty of disabilities that need correcting, including mine. At the same time, I know that Leah and I, and the millions of other people living with genetic disorders, bring a multitude of gifts into the human family, some of which are valuable precisely because they were forged in the crucible of our pain and suffering.

My story of living with OI, raising a beloved child with OI, and making reproductive decisions in light of OI really encompasses several stories. In one story, OI is a basic brokenness in need of fixing. In another, OI is just one of many human limitations in need of acceptance. When Leah is in the emergency room with a new fracture—drugged and defeated, yet receiving skilled, compassionate treatment from doctors and nurses who have made sick children their life's mission—I can believe the story about the miraculous ability of modern medicine to fix problems that used to be unfixable. Or I can believe the story about the pain that no amount of drugs or toys or soothing words can banish. In reality, I believe each of those stories at different times, and sometimes several at once. My perspective on reproductive technology is influenced by these conflicting stories.

In Yann Martel's novel *The Life of Pi*, the main character describes the crucial role of the stories we tell to make sense of our lives. Pi, an Indian boy, is the only human survivor of a shipwreck. He ends up in a lifeboat with several zoo animals, including a Bengal tiger he names Richard Parker. When Pi is rescued and tells his story, his tale is met with unbelief. So he tells a different story, in which he was on the lifeboat with his mother, a cannibalistic cook, and a sailor, all of whom die in various grisly ways. The ultimate question of the book is, Which story do you believe? Both stories are frightening and full of death, but one—the one with the tiger—also tells of mystery, hope, and miracle. Early in the book, Pi writes:

> I can well imagine an atheist's last words: "White, white! L-L-Love! My God!"—and the deathbed leap of faith. Whereas the agnostic, if he stays true to his reasonable self, if he stays beholden to dry, yeastless factuality, might try to explain the warm light bathing him by saying, "Possibly a f-f-failing oxygenation of the b-b-brain," and, to the very end, lack imagination and miss the better story.

For Christians, one story—about the life, death, and resurrection of Jesus Christ—prevails over all the hurts and joys that influence how we frame our life story on any given day. Being a Christian is about continually and consciously choosing to believe that hope, healing, and life conquer despair, brokenness, and death no matter what each day brings. Christian faith is ultimately an invitation to believe the better story, about a God who fixes what is broken, heals what is hurt, and brings what is dead to life. That is the story I cling to, and to which I turn when I'm trying to make sense of my childbearing decisions and the promise and peril of reproductive technologies. The Christian narrative does not provide an obvious answer to whether it's ethically sound for believers to use IVF, PGD, or other assisted reproduction techniques. But it does provide a grounded, hopeful context in which to ponder essential questions about whether and how we will bear children as technology offers us ever-more-sophisticated techniques to do so. Infertility and family legacies of genetic disease inevitably cause substantial pain, but the Christian story invites us, even while we are mired in that pain, to believe in and cling to the extremity of love.

Notes

INTRODUCTION

IVF leads to live birth of infants about 30 percent of the time. —The 30 percent figure comes from 2008 Centers for Disease Control Data, http://www.cdc.gov/art/ART2008/index.htm.

Have four million births through IVF trumped all the moral and ethical questions that were posed by the procedure? —Robert Siegel, *The Ethics of In Vitro Fertilization*, in an interview with Jeffrey Kahn on National Public Radio, October 4, 2010.

Their parents were overjoyed to be able to start a family. —Nicholas Wade, "Pioneer of In Vitro Fertilization Wins Nobel Prize," *The New York Times*, October 4, 2010.

Soon it will be a sin of parents to have a child that carries the heavy burden of genetic disease. We are entering a world where we have to consider the quality of our children. —Lois Rogers, "Having Disabled Babies Will Be 'Sin,' Says Scientist," *Sunday Times* (London), July 4, 1999.

A few memoirists. —See, for example, Laurie Strongin's memoir *Saving Henry: A Mother's Journey* (New York: Hyperion, 2010) and Bonnie J. Rough's memoir *Carrier: Untangling the Danger in My DNA* (Berkeley, CA: Counterpoint, 2010), both written by mothers who made childbearing decisions in light of having a serious genetic disorder in their family history.

CHAPTER 1: FEAR OF FALLING

Any aspect of that extra chromosome causing separation—physical, emotional, relational—will be overcome. —Amy Julia Becker, "Babies Perfect and Imperfect," posted on *First Things: On the Square*, November 2008, http://www.firstthings.com/article/2008/10/001-babies-perfect-and-imperfect-23.

Product of societal norms rather than of problems intrinsic to the disabilities themselves. —Amy Julia Becker, "The Good Life," posted on *First Things: On the Square*, December 31, 2008, http://www.firstthings.com/onthesquare/2008/12/the-good-life.

The result of our unwillingness to change our lives so that those disabled might have a better life. —Stanley Hauerwas, "Suffering the Retarded: Should We Prevent Retardation?" *Journal of Religion, Disability, and Health* 8, nos. 3–4 (2004): 90–100; this article was written in the 1980s, before the terms "retardation" and "the retarded" were perceived as derogatory and outdated.

Disability is just disability, period.—Online comment in response to Ellen Painter Dollar, "I Want to Be Accepted as I Am, but I'll Take a Cure Too," posted on *Christianity Today: Speaking Out*, February 15, 2010, http://www.christianitytoday.com/ct/2010/februaryweb-only/17.11.0.html.

Suffering and death, considered in themselves, have no ultimate meaning at all. —David B. Hart, "Tsunami and Theodicy," posted on *First Things: On the Square*, January 15, 2010, http://www.firstthings.com/onthesquare/2010/01/tsunami-and-theodicy.

A discussion of whether, if it becomes possible to cure Down syndrome, we should cure Down syndrome. —See Lisa Belkin, "Should Down Syndrome Be Cured?" posted on *Motherlode: Adventures in Parenting*, January 11, 2010, http://parenting.blogs.nytimes.com/2010/01/11/should-down-syndrome-be-cured/; Rod Dreher, "Would You Cure Your Kid's Down Syndrome?" posted on *Rod Dreher: Science, Religion, Markets, and Morals*, January 28, 2010, http://blog.beliefnet.com/roddreher/2010/01/would-you-cure-your-kids-down-syndrome.html; and Amy Julia Becker, "Considering 'Curing' Down Syndrome with Caution," posted on *Christianity Today: Speaking Out*, February 12, 2010, http://www.christianitytoday.com/ct/2010/februaryweb-only/16-51.0.html.

An example of how the world is not as it should be. —Dollar, "I Want to Be Accepted."

Thus our suffering even makes us unsure of who we are. —Hauerwas, "Suffering the Retarded," 102.

I've been entirely comfortable in my own skin. —Harriet McBryde Johnson, "Unspeakable Conversations," *The New York Times Magazine*, February 16, 2003, 25.

I want to be accepted as I am, but I'll take a cure too. —Dollar, "I Want to Be Accepted."

Platitudes such as . . . —I believe that "God will not give you more than you can handle" is a distortion of 1 Corinthians 10:13, which says that God will not let you be tempted (or tested) beyond what you can bear. I object to the implication that God gives us illness and disability as tests, after first evaluating whether we'll handle them gracefully. I do not accept that these things come directly from God in the first place, and I find it hard to believe in a God who says to one family, "I'm going to test *you* with a few months of unemployment," and to another, "I'm going to test *you* by giving your child a fatal genetic disorder. But I know you can handle it!" Having married into a family grieving over several suicides, I also think there is abundant evidence that many people are burdened with more than they can handle. As Episcopal chaplain Marshall Scott has written about this 1 Corinthians passage, "The point is that when we are tested by all the things that flesh is heir to, God will be with us, and will provide us what we need to endure." See Marshall Scott, "I've Been Having a Hard Time with This, Chaplain," posted on the *Daily Episcopalian*. March 23, 2010, http://www.episcopalcafe.com/daily/health/by _marshall_scott_ive_been.php.

A scourge which we will neither accept nor try to explain in some positive sense. —Hauerwas, "Suffering the Retarded," 95.

One that makes life's goodness dependent upon "choice," the other that makes life's goodness dependent upon "gift." —Hans Reinders, "Life's Goodness: On Disability, Genetics, and 'Choice,'" in *Theology, Disability, and the New Genetics: Why Science Needs the Church*, ed. John Swinton and Brian Brock (New York: Continuum, 2007), 164.

If my life were different from what it happens to be, then it would also be good. —Ibid., 169.

Straighter line to God. —Online comment in response to Amy Julia Becker, "Eliminating Suffering or Eliminating People?" posted on *Her.meneutics: Christianity Today Blog for Women*, February 26, 2010, http://blog.christianitytoday.com/women/2010/02/eliminating_suffering_or_elimi.html.

I would have an abortion. —Ayelet Waldman, *Bad Mother: A Chronicle of Maternal Crimes, Minor Calamities, and Occasional Moments of Grace* (New York: Doubleday, 2009), 127.

CHAPTER 2: SETTING OUT

Some of the hormones used for fertility treatment were harvested from the urine of a bunch of Italian nuns. —The Italian drug company Serono (now known as Merck Serono) started developing fertility drugs in the mid-twentieth century by collecting follicle-stimulating hormone (FSH) from the urine of postmenopausal women. Italian women reportedly donated their urine as an altruistic gesture, similar to blood donation. Some sources claim that Italian nuns were among those who participated in the urine collections, while other sources call these reports "folklore." At an information session for prospective patients, our fertility doctor showed a photo of a group of nuns on a picturesque Italian street, with plastic jugs of urine awaiting pickup.

Psychosocial reasons for childbearing. —See, for example, F. Van Balen and T. C. M. Trimbos-Kemper, "Involuntarily Childless Couples: Their Desire to Have Children and Their Motives," *Journal of Psychosomatic Obstetrics and Gynecology* 16 (1995): 137–44; and Yvonne Wesley, "Why Women Want Children: Defining the Meaning of Desire for Children and the Construction of an Index," *Journal of the National Black Nurses Association* 18, no. 1 (2007): 14–20.

Studies have shown that women. —Van Balen and Tribos-Kemper, "Involuntarily Childless Couples," 141, 143.

Women often perceive motherhood. —Wesley, "Why Women Want Children," 15.

Mary Gordon's writing on pregnancy —Christine E. Gudorf, "Dissecting Parenthood: Infertility, In Vitro, and Other Lessons in Why and How We Parent," *Conscience* 15, no. 3 (Autumn 1994): 17.

Addiction to pregnancy and lactation. —Ibid.

Humans, or many humans, have an overpowering need to have—to be—a family. —Liza Mundy, *Everything Conceivable: How Assisted Reproduction Is Changing the World* (New York: Alfred A. Knopf, 2007), 342.

The sexual appetite and instinctive drives to reproduce are a gift from God. —Anna Poulson, "Maybe Baby," *Third Way* 26, no. 2 (2003): 12–14.

Having children as a vocation is rather different than regarding them as a choice. —Ibid., 13.

The Roman Catholic Church's opposition to all forms of assisted reproduction. —Two recent statements reaffirming the Catholic position on assisted reproduction are from the Congregation for the Doctrine of the Faith, *Instruction "Dignitas Personae" on Certain Bioethical Questions*, September 8, 2008, http://www.vatican.va/roman_curia/congregations/cfaith/documents/rc_con_cfaith_doc_20081212_sintesi-dignitas-personae_en.html; and the U.S. Conference of Catholic Bishops, *Life-Giving Love in an Age of Technology*, November 17, 2009, http://www.usccb.org/LifeGivingLove/lifegivinglovedocument.pdf.

Distinction between procreation and reproduction. —Gilbert Meilaender, *Bioethics: A Primer for Christians* (Grand Rapids: Wm. B. Eerdmans Publishing Co., 1996), 14–15.

The call to adoption is almost always applied selectively. —Maura A. Ryan, *Ethics and Economics of Assisted Reproduction: The Cost of Longing* (Washington, DC: Georgetown University Press, 2001), 57.

There have never been enough adoptable children. —Mundy, *Everything Conceivable*, 45.

A myth of unwanted children. —Paul Lauritzen, *Pursuing Parenthood: Ethical Issues in Assisted Reproduction* (Bloomington: Indiana University Press, 1993), 126.

The last thing children traumatized by the earthquake needed was to travel to an unfamiliar place. —Lisa Belkin, "Adopting a Child from Haiti," posted on *Motherlode: Adventures in Parenting*, January 25, 2010, http://parenting.blogs.nytimes.com/2010/01/25/adopting-a-child-from-haiti/.

Voluntary relinquishment of Haitian children. —David Gauthier-Villars, Miriam Jordan, and Joel Millman, "Earthquake Exposes Haiti's Faulty Adoption System," *The Wall Street Journal*, February 27, 2010, http://online.wsj.com/article/SB10001424052748704625004575089521195349384.html?mod=WSJ_World_MIDDLENews.

Emotional realities of adoption. —Online comment to Ellen Painter Dollar, "'Why Don't You Just Adopt'? The Frequent Question Assumes That Adoption Is Both Easy and Morally Superior," posted on *Her.meneutics: The Christianity Today*

Blog for Women, March 9, 2010, http://blog.christianitytoday.com/women/2010/03/why_dont_you_just_adopt_1.html.

Every adoption involves loss. —Lauritzen, *Pursuing Parenthood*, 129–30.

Parents can no longer enter into parenthood blithely and unreflectively. —Bonnie J. Miller-McLemore, "'Let the Children Come' Revisited," in *The Child in Christian Thought*, ed. Marcia J. Bunge (Grand Rapids: Wm. B. Eerdmans Publishing Co., 2001), 465.

Unconditional love is a signal requirement of being a parent. —Mundy, *Everything Conceivable*, 321.

CHAPTER 3: WITHOUT A MAP

PGD did not make our risk of other genetic anomalies greater. —As of this writing, there is no conclusive evidence that either IVF or PGD causes significant health problems in babies conceived via these technologies. However, some studies suggest that genetic changes appearing in babies conceived through IVF could raise their risk of problems such as diabetes and obesity. It is unclear whether these genetic changes are caused by IVF or perhaps are already present in the parents' sperm and/or eggs and possibly related to their infertility. There is also some preliminary evidence that IVF may allow baby boys to inherit their father's infertility, as well as some increased risks of other genetic problems that occur together with certain types of male infertility. All of these studies, however, are preliminary, and these potential problems did not apply in our case because we were not infertile.

The increased chance we would have twins. —In the years since our PGD/IVF attempt, clinicians have adopted voluntary guidelines for the number of embryos to transfer in IVF cycles, in an attempt to stem rising rates of multiple pregnancies. American Society for Reproductive Medicine guidelines now recommend that for a woman my age (I was under thirty-five at the time), only one embryo should be transferred. But these guidelines were not in place when we were undergoing IVF, and even now, compliance is voluntary, not required. Our doctors never raised the option of transferring only one embryo (assuming we would have several OI-free embryos to choose from), and the idea never crossed our minds. We wanted to maximize our chances of success, knowing that we might not be able to afford more than one cycle, and we understood that transferring multiple embryos was standard practice.

You have helped me imagine a different way of seeing reproductive technology. —E-mail from Christopher C. Roberts to Ellen Painter Dollar, Saturday, May 18, 2002.

Responding directly to people's unique stories is vital. —Only after I was long into the process of writing this book did I learn the name for ethical reflection that honors individuals' stories: narrative ethics. Advocates for a narrative approach argue that it transforms ethics from a stand-alone, juridical process, in which experts weigh the merits of various arguments based on ethical theory and render a judgment—to a communal, consensus-building process, in which amateurs grapple with the stories on both sides of a bioethical debate, accepting their emotional complexity and constructing "new ways of living well together." Hilde Undemann Nelson, "Context: Backward, Sideways, and Forward," in *Stories Matter: The Role of Narrative in Medical Ethics*, ed. Rita Charon and Martha Montello (New York: Routledge, 2002), 46.

This is your suffering. —E-mail from Christopher C. Roberts to Ellen Painter Dollar, March 28, 2002.

Minimizing your children's suffering is not the same as good parenting. —E-mail from Christopher C. Roberts to Daniel Dollar, March 26, 2002.

I know avoiding suffering is not what God calls us to, but it sure does sound nice. —E-mail from Ellen Painter Dollar to Christopher C. Roberts, March 26, 2002.

I realized how deeply I desired freedom from OI. —E-mail from Ellen Painter Dollar to Christopher C. Roberts, May 17, 2002.

This particular brand of heartache has worn out its welcome in my life. —Ibid.

Determining the outcome is exactly what cannot be done. —Liza Mundy, *Everything Conceivable: How Assisted Reproduction Is Changing the World* (New York: Alfred A. Knopf, 2007), 332.

PGD is generally acceptable for Jewish couples. —See, for example, Fred Rosner, "Judaism, Genetic Screening, and Genetic Therapy," posted on *Jewish Virtual Library*, http://www.jewishvirtuallibrary.org/jsource/Judaism/genetic.html.

The new science would take off race and class blinders. —Amy Laura Hall, *Conceiving Parenthood: American Protestantism and the Spirit of Reproduction* (Grand Rapids: Wm. B. Eerdmans, 2008), 271.

Osgood's sermon on God the Refiner. —Ibid., 260–62.

Lysol used to prevent pregnancy. —Ibid., 75–78.

Justification by meticulously planned procreation. —Ibid., 10, with original emphasis.

Episcopalians' procreative restraint. —Deborah Solomon, "State of the Church: Questions for Katharine Jefferts Schori," *New York Times Magazine*, November 19, 2006, http://www.nytimes.com/2006/11/19/magazine/19WWLN_Q4.html?pagewanted=print.

Hall's interviews with modern women on parenting pressures. —Hall, *Conceiving Parenthood*, 3–4.

Pregnancies that seem inadequately planned. —Ibid., 4.

We are entering a world where we have to consider the quality of our children. —Lois Rogers, "Having Disabled Babies Will Be 'Sin,' Says Scientist," *Sunday Times* (London), July 4, 1999.

We are not commodities to be bought and sold. —John Swinton, "Introduction: Re-imagining Genetics and Disability," in *Theology, Disability, and the New Genetics: Why Science Needs the Church*, ed. John Swinton and Brian Brock (New York: Continuum, 2007), 11.

Stories as a valuable resource. —One of the most perspective-changing stories I've come across is Laurie Strongin's memoir *Saving Henry: A Mother's Journey* (New York: Hyperion, 2010). Strongin and her husband went through nine PGD attempts to conceive a so-called savior sibling for their son Henry, who had a fatal genetic blood disorder. Through PGD, they hoped to conceive another child who would be free of the same blood disorder and also be a donor match for Henry, so they could use the baby's umbilical cord stem cells to provide Henry with a lifesaving bone-marrow transplant. None of the PGD cycles worked, although the couple did have two additional sons conceived naturally; neither son inherited the disorder, but neither was a good donor match for Henry, who died when he was seven. On the surface this story appears to epitomize the commodification of children; here, after all, are parents who wanted to conceive a child with very specific qualities for a very specific purpose. But after reading their story, I found it impossible to accuse this family of treating their children as products subject to quality control. Henry's parents have become outspoken advocates not only for PGD but also against the use of this technology to select for superficial, nondisease traits.

The quest for the perfect offspring was a goal since antiquity. —Randi Hutter Epstein, *Get Me Out: A History of Childbirth from the Garden of Eden to the Sperm Bank* (New York: W. W. Norton, 2010), xiii.

Many fertility patients are deeply grateful for what they get. —Mundy, *Everything Conceivable*, 18.

Dayna Olson-Getty's story. —Dayna's blog is at www.daynasmusings.blogspot.com. See especially her post "In Life and Death" (December 27, 2009), which tells the story of her son's birth and death; and her post "Photos of Our Beautiful Boy" (September 6, 2009).

Complete freedom, godlike freedom, gives rise to utter responsibility. —Gilbert Meilaender, *Bioethics: A Primer for Christians* (Grand Rapids: Wm. B. Eerdmans Publishing Co., 1996), 55.

We would have lost that baby, but we would not have killed that baby. —Bill Keller, "Charlie's Ghost," *The New York Times Magazine*, June 29, 2002.

The technology carries its own momentum. —Meilaender, *Bioethics*, 55.

CHAPTER 4: THE SLIPPERY SLOPE

I was also making a deal—and they were making a buck. —Peggy Orenstein, *Waiting for Daisy: A Tale of Two Continents, Three Religions, Five Infertility Doctors, an Oscar, an Atomic Bomb, a Romantic Night, and One Woman's Quest to Become a Mother* (New York: Bloomsbury, 2007), 193.

Debora Spar on supply and demand in the fertility business. —Claudia Dreifus, "An Economist Examines the Business of Fertility," *The New York Times*, February 28, 2006.

Voluntary guidelines on the number of embryos to transfer in an IVF cycle. —American Society for Reproductive Medicine, "Guidelines on Number of Embryos Transferred," *Fertility and Sterility* 92, no. 5 (November 2009): 1518–19.

Why voluntary guidelines are regularly ignored. —Stephanie Saul, "The Gift of Life, and Its Price," *The New York Times*, October 10, 2009.

Fertility specialists' salaries at major universities. —Tamar Lewin, "Many Specialists at Private Universities Earn More Than Presidents," *The New York Times*, February 22, 2009.

Guidelines on egg-donor compensation often ignored. —Aaron D. Levine, "Self-Regulation, Compensation, and the Ethical Recruitment of Oocyte Donors," *Hastings Center Report* 40, no. 2 (2010): 25–36.

Controversy over proposed plan to offer PGD to select for eye and hair color. —Laura Bauer, "California Fertility Doctor's Offer of Trait Selection Stirs Ethical Questions," *Kansas City Star*, March 3, 2009.

What is at work in assisted reproduction is often not science but business. —Liza Mundy, *Everything Conceivable: How Assisted Reproduction Is Changing the World* (New York: Alfred A. Knopf, 2007), 332.

No federally funded experiments could be conducted on the safety and efficacy of IVF. —Ibid., 33.

The Indian government is considering more oversight of fertility clinics. —Hillary Brenhouse, "India's Rent-a-Womb Industry Faces New Restrictions," *Time*, June 5, 2010.

Maybe he just needs a little time to get used to the idea of using two surrogates. —Having two babies born of two different gestational surrogates at the same time was the subject of a *New York Times Magazine* cover article on December 29, 2010. Writer Melanie Thernstrom detailed her and her husband's decision to pursue parenthood via egg donation and gestational surrogate because Thernstrom was already in her 40s when they got married. They ended up having two babies, a boy and a girl, born of two different surrogates five days apart. Thernstrom refers to her children as the "Twiblings." See Melanie Therstrom, "Meet the Twiblings," *New York Times Magazine*, December 29, 2010; and Ellen Painter Dollar, "Troubled by the Twiblings?" posted on *Her.meneutics: The Christianity Today Blog for Women*, January 23, 2011, http://blog.christianitytoday.com/women/2011/01/what_do_you_call_two.html.

What was with these guys? —Orenstein, *Waiting for Daisy*, 85.

The very availability of the technology appears to exert a sort of tyrannical pressure to use it. —Paul Lauritzen, *Pursuing Parenthood: Ethical Issues in Assisted Reproduction* (Bloomington: Indiana University Press, 1993), xiv.

It becomes difficult to judge various technological manipulations . . . by criteria other than the likelihood of success. —Ibid., 20.

Termination rates for fetuses prenatally diagnosed with Down syndrome are around 90 percent. —See, for example, Caroline Mansfield et al., "Termination

Rates after Prenatal Diagnosis of Down Syndrome, Spina Bifida, Anencephaly, and Turner and Klinefelter Syndromes: A Systematic Literature Review," *Prenatal Diagnosis* 19 (1999): 808–12.

Physicians provided parents with incomplete information about Down syndrome. —Keri Steadman, "Understanding the Implications of Prenatal Testing for Down Syndrome," September 14, 2009, article at the Children's Hospital Boston News Room, http://www.eurekalert.org/pub_releases/2009-09/chb-uti091409.php.

Need for doctors to offer more up-to-date information and referral to support groups. —Brian G. Skotko, "Prenatally Diagnosed Down Syndrome: Mothers Who Continued Their Pregnancies Evaluate Their Health Care Providers," *American Journal of Obstetrics and Gynecology* 192, no. 3 (March 2005): 670–77.

Doctors and genetic counselors emphasize the option to terminate pregnancies. —Julia Duin, "Choosing Not to Abort Babies with Disabilities," *Washington Times*, May 10, 2009.

Our first experience of being offered medical treatment which we neither sought nor desired. —Brian Brock and Stephanie Brock, "Being Disabled in the New World of Genetic Testing: A Snapshot of Shifting Landscapes," In *Theology, Disability, and the New Genetics: Why Science Needs the Church* (New York: Continuum, 2007), 31.

Simply having *genetic testing has shifted medical behavior toward the disabled.* —Ibid., 34.

Doctors have a skewed perception of the suffering that comes along with certain disabilities. —Author's interview with Amy Julia Becker, June 10, 2010.

You know you've arrived in a different universe when the word "fatal" comes as a relief. —Jonathan Tropper, "Good-bye Too Soon," *The New York Times Magazine*, March 6, 2005.

A shocking refusal to accept that gravely disabled people can experience happiness or bring it to others. —Melanie Phillips, "The Hospital Gods Who Decide Whether We Die," *Sunday Times* (London), July 25, 1999. The Edwards quote she was responding to appeared in Lois Rogers, "Having Disabled Babies Will Be 'Sin,' Says Scientist," *Sunday Times* (London), July 4, 1999.

PGD used by parents who don't want to undergo prenatal diagnosis because they would never choose pregnancy termination. —Mundy, *Everything Conceivable*, 322.

PGD as primary preventive medicine. —Yuri Verlinsky and Anver Kuliev, "Ethical, Social, and Legal Issues," in *Practical Preimplantation Genetic Diagnosis* (London: Springer-Verlag, 2005), 189.

It is far easier for humans, whatever their ethical and religious beliefs, to reject embryos than to abort fetuses. —Masha Gessen, *Blood Matters: From Inherited Illness to Designer Babies; How the World and I Found Ourselves in the Future of the Gene* (New York: Harcourt, 2008), 268.

Responsible to ensure that future generations will not be faced with the same difficulties. —Verlinsky and Kuliev, "Ethical, Social, and Legal Issues," 191.

PGD is a natural evolution of assisted reproduction. —Ibid., 193.

The ability of modern medicine to cure is at once a benefit and potential pitfall. —Stanley Hauerwas, "Salvation and Health: Why Medicine Needs the Church," in *On Moral Medicine*, ed. Stephen E. Lammers and Allen Verhey (Grand Rapids: Wm. B. Eerdmans Publishing Co., 1998), 75.

Genetic normality is surely a contradiction in terms. —Phillips, "The Hospital Gods."

Contemporary medicine finds itself in a framework of fear rather than gratitude. —Brock and Brock, "Being Disabled," 41.

CHAPTER 5: WHAT IS LOST ALONG THE WAY

60 Minutes story on families using PGD —For a written version of the stories told on *60 Minutes*, see Rebecca Leung, "Choose the Sex of Your Baby: New Technology May Allow Couples to Design the Perfect Baby," April 14, 2004, on the *CBS News* Web site, http://www.cbsnews.com/stories/2004/08/09/60II/main634979.shtml?tag=mncol;lst;3.

Provide better resources for prospective parents. —Ellen Painter Dollar, "First, Help Couples," *Christianity Today*, July 2010, 47.

Other answers to question concerning leftover embryos after IVF. —Ron Stoddart, "Adopt Them," *Christianity Today*, July 2010, 46; and David Cook, "Take Responsibility," *Christianity Today*, July 2010, 46–47.

Donor-conceived adults carry more uncertainty about their identity. —Elizabeth Marquardt, Norval D. Glenn, and Karen Clark, *My Daddy's Name Is Donor: A New Study of Young Adults Conceived through Sperm Donation* (New York: Institute for American Values, 2010).

The authors reduce moral deliberation to procedural thoroughness. —William Cutrer and Sandra Glahn, *When Empty Arms Become a Heavy Burden: Encouragement for Couples Facing Infertility* (Grand Rapids: Kregel), 2010.

Whether every choice made possible by science is a choice pro-choicers should welcome. —Liza Mundy, *Everything Conceivable: How Assisted Reproduction Is Changing the World* (New York: Alfred A. Knopf), 2007, 314.

Reproductive liberty can be, and is, invoked by fertility doctors. —Ibid., 318.

U.S. clinics marketing sex-selection services to people of Indian and Chinese descent. —Viji Sundaram, "Oh, No, It's a Girl! South Asians Flock to Sex-Selection Clinics in the U.S.," *New American Media*, August 31. 2010, http://newamericamedia.org/2010/08/oh-no-its-a-girl-south-asians-flock-to-sex-selection-clinics-in-us.php.

There were lots of women looking forward to dressing little girls in pink outfits. —Mundy, *Everything Conceivable*, 318–19.

Any effort to direct any reproductive decision made by any individual is to call into question all decisions made by all individuals, including, of course, the decision to abort. —Ibid., 319.

Ad campaign takes literally the idea of a fetus as a person. —Tracy Clark-Flory, "The Comedy of 'Fetal Personhood': A New Ad Lampoons These Anti-Abortion Initiatives by Interpreting Them Literally," *Salon*, October 4, 2010, http://www.salon.com/life/broadsheet/2010/10/04/fetal_personhood/index.html.

Whether we know confidently or are agnostic about the status of thirteen-day-old embryos. —E-mail from Christopher C. Roberts to Ellen Painter Dollar, March 26, 2002.

The element of chance is one of the factors which most distinguish the act of begetting from the act of technique. —Oliver O'Donovan, "In a Glass Darkly," in *On Moral Medicine*, ed. Stephen E. Lammers and Allen Verhey (Grand Rapids: Wm. B. Eerdmans Publishing Co., 1998), 498.

Avoid the temptation to "fetishize nature." —Mundy, *Everything Conceivable*, 85.

What I'd experienced had not been a full life, nor was it a full death, but it was a real loss. —Peggy Orenstein, *Waiting for Daisy: A Tale of Two Continents, Three Religions, Five Infertility Doctors, an Oscar, an Atomic Bomb, a Romantic Night, and One Woman's Quest to Become a Mother* (New York: Bloomsbury, 2007), 139.

Definition of mizuko. —Ibid., 134–35.

In the political discussion, there has been no vocabulary of nuance. —Peggy Orenstein, "Mourning My Miscarriage," *The New York Times Magazine*, April 21, 2002.

The technology that informs you [that] your future baby is mysteriously endangered also makes him real. —Bill Keller, "Charlie's Ghost," *The New York Times Magazine*, June 29, 2002.

Contemplating the fate of their embryos was harder than their decision to go forward with the donor oocyte [and IVF] procedure itself. —Robert D. Nachtigall, Gay Becker, Carrie Friese, Anneliese Butler, and Kirstin MacDougall, "Parents' Conceptualization of Their Frozen Embryos Complicates the Disposition Decision," *Fertility and Sterility* 84, no. 5 (August 2005): 431–34, esp. 431.

The complex nature of the couples' conceptualization of their embryos. —Ibid., 433.

Instead, her disabilities have exposed our common humanity. —Amy Julia Becker, "Sometimes It's Good Not to Have a Choice (or What I Didn't Know Didn't Hurt Me)," posted on *Thin Places: Amy Julia Becker on Faith, Family, and Disability*, May 7, 2011.

PGD and prenatal diagnosis do not devalue people with disabilities. —Janet Malek, "Deciding against Disability: Does the Use of Reproductive Genetic Technologies Express Disvalue for People with Disabilities?" *Journal of Medical Ethics* 36 (2010): 217–21.

Couples more focused on getting pregnant than on the decisions that might follow. —Nachtigall et al., "Parents' Conceptualization," 433.

CHAPTER 6: WHERE WE ENDED UP

Shouldn't we always be prepared to welcome the difference and potential difficulty of a child? —Author's interview with Melissa Florer-Bixler, April 7, 2010.

Decision to pursue only noninvasive prenatal tests solely for medically relevant information. —Amy Julia Becker, "Why Prenatal Testing Harms as Much as It Helps," posted on the *New York Times* Motherlode blog, September 14, 2010, http://parenting.blogs.nytimes.com/2010/09/14/deciding-not-to-screen-for-down-syndrome/.

CHAPTER 7: "THE ONLY WAY IS HARD"

Bioethics class talking about couple who tested for Down syndrome and did selective reduction of IVF pregnancy. —Tod Chambers and Kathryn Montgomery, "Plot: Framing Contingency and Choice in Bioethics," in *Stories Matter: The Role of Narrative in Medical Ethics*, ed. Rita Charon and Maria Montello (New York: Routledge, 2002), 90-91.

Case study of sixty-year-old woman requesting IVF. —Susan B. Rubin, "Beyond the Authoritative Voice: Casting a Wide Net in Ethics Consultation," in Charon and Montello, *Stories Matter*, 109–18.

It is in the dialogue, and there alone. —Charles Anderson and Maria Montello, "The Reader's Response and Why It Matters in Biomedical Ethics," in Charon and Montello, *Stories Matter*, 93.

Voluntary postponement of childbearing. —Gillian E. St. Lawrence. "By Freezing Embryos, Couples Try to Utilize Fertility While Delaying Parenthood," *The Washington Post*, July 6, 2010.

Grandmother gives birth to grandson. —Deborah L. Shelton, "Woman, 61, Gives Birth to Own Grandchild," *Chicago Tribune*, February 11, 2011.

Clinic personnel insisted they were simply offering a medical service to a needy clientele. —Rob Stein, "London Seminar Offering Free IVF from Virginia Clinic Sparks Controversy," *The Washington Post*, March 18, 2010.

[Reproductive] technology carries its own momentum. —Gilbert Meilaender, *Bioethics: A Primer for Christians* (Grand Rapids: Wm. B. Eerdmans Publishing Co., 1996), 55.

The Religious Institute calls on religious leaders to more effectively support congregants coping with reproductive decisions. —Kate Ott, *A Time to Be Born: A Faith-Based Guide to Reproductive Technologies* (Westport, CT: The Religious Institute), 2009.

Finding a careful balance between personal autonomy and the public welfare is often a considerable challenge. —Jacob M. Appel, "Motherhood: Is It Ever Too

Late?" posted on *The Huffington Post*, July 15, 2009, http://www.huffingtonpost
.com/jacob-m-appel/motherhood-is-it-ever-too_b_233916.html.

Calling IVF-conceived children "undignified." —Jenny Minton, *The Early
Birds: A Mother's Story for Our Times* (New York: Alfred A. Knopf, 2006), 206.

*Troubling word choices in U.S. Catholic bishops' document on reproductive
technology.* —U.S. Conference of Catholic Bishops, *Life-Giving Love in an Age of
Technology*, November 17, 2009, http://www.usccb.org/LifeGivingLove/lifegiving
lovedocument.pdf.

The spouses have decided not to be fully the mother and father of their child.
—Ibid., 5.

Reproductive technology "violates" a marriage. —Ibid.

*Many couples find that their marriage is stronger at the end of their reproduc-
tive journeys.* —See, for example, a post on my *Choices That Matter* blog titled "An
Unexpected Path to Surrogacy," posted on February 23 and 24, 2011, http://choices
thatmatter.blogspot.com/2011/02/stories-matteran-unexpected-path-to_24.html.

For Further Reading

Elise Erikson Barrett. *What Was Lost: A Christian Journey through Miscarriage.* Louisville, KY: Westminster John Knox Press, 2010.

Martha Beck. *Expecting Adam: A True Story of Birth, Rebirth, and Everyday Magic.* New York: Berkley Pub., 2000.

Amy Julia Becker. "Considering 'Curing' Down Syndrome with Caution." Posted on *Christianity Today: Speaking Out.* February 12, 2010. http://www.christianitytoday.com/ct/2010/februaryweb-only/16-51.0.html.

———. *A Good and Perfect Gift: Faith, Expectations, and a Little Girl Named Penny.* Ada, MI: Bethany House, 2011.

Brian Brock and Stephanie Brock. "Being Disabled in the New World of Genetic Testing: A Snapshot of Shifting Landscapes." In *Theology, Disability, and the New Genetics: Why Science Needs the Church,* edited by John Swinton and Brian Brock, 29–43. New York: Continuum, 2007.

Marcia J. Bunge, ed. *The Child in Christian Thought.* Grand Rapids: Wm. B. Eerdmans Publishing Co., 2001.

Rita Charon and Martha Montello, eds. *Stories Matter: The Role of Narrative in Medical Ethics.* New York: Routledge, 2002.

Congregation for the Doctrine of the Faith. *Instruction "Dignitas Personae" on Certain Bioethical Questions.* September 8, 2008. http://www.vatican.va/roman_curia/congregations/cfaith/documents/rc_con_cfaith_doc_20081212_sintesi-dignitas-personae-en.html.

———. *Instruction "Donum Vitae" on Respect for Human Life in Its Origin and on the Dignity of Procreation.* February 22, 1987. http://www.vatican.va/roman_curia/congregations/cfaith/documents/rc_con_cfaith_doc_19870222_respect-for-human-life_en.html.

Ellen Painter Dollar. "First, Help Couples." *Christianity Today.* July 2010. http://www.christianitytoday.com/ct/2010/july/27.46.html.

———. "I Want to Be Accepted as I Am, but I'll Take a Cure Too." Posted on *Christianity Today: Speaking Out.* February 15, 2010. http://www.christianitytoday.com/ct/2010/februaryweb-only/17.11.0.html.

Randi Hutter Epstein. *Get Me Out: A History of Childbirth from the Garden of Eden to the Sperm Bank*. New York: W. W. Norton, 2010.

Masha Gessen. *Blood Matters: From Inherited Illness to Designer Babies; How the World and I Found Ourselves in the Future of the Gene*. New York: Harcourt, 2008.

Jennifer Grant. *Love You More: The Divine Surprise of Adopting My Daughter*. Nashville: Thomas Nelson, 2011.

Christine E. Gudorf. "Dissecting Parenthood: Infertility, In Vitro, and Other Lessons in Why and How We Parent." *Conscience* 15, no. 3 (Autumn 1994): 15–22.

Debra W. Haffner and Timothy Palmer. *Sexuality and Religion 2020: Goals for the Next Decade*. Westport, CT: The Religious Institute, 2010.

Amy Laura Hall. *Conceiving Parenthood: American Protestantism and the Spirit of Reproduction*. Grand Rapids: Wm. B. Eerdmans Publishing Co., 2008.

Stanley Hauerwas. "Salvation and Health: Why Medicine Needs the Church." In *On Moral Medicine*, edited by Stephen E. Lammers and Allen Verhey, 72–83. Grand Rapids: Wm. B. Eerdmans Publishing Co., 1998.

———. "Suffering the Retarded: Should We Prevent Retardation?" *Journal of Religion, Disability and Health* 8, nos. 3–4 (2004): 87–106.

Aldous Huxley. *Brave New World*. New York: Harper Perennial, 2006.

Harriet McBryde Johnson. "Unspeakable Conversations." *The New York Times Magazine*. February 16, 2003.

Bill Keller. "Charlie's Ghost." *The New York Times Magazine*. June 29, 2002.

Stephen E. Lammers and Allen Verhey, eds. *On Moral Medicine*. Grand Rapids: Wm. B. Eerdmans Publishing Co., 1998.

Paul Lauritzen. *Pursuing Parenthood: Ethical Issues in Assisted Reproduction*. Bloomington: Indiana University Press, 1993.

Lois Lowry. *The Giver*. New York: Delacorte Books for Young Readers, 2006.

M. Therese Lysaught. "From Clinic to Congregation: Religious Communities and Genetic Medicine." In *On Moral Medicine*, edited by Stephen E. Lammers and Allen Verhey, 547–61. Grand Rapids: Wm. B. Eerdmans Publishing Co., 1998.

Janet Malek. "Deciding against Disability: Does the Use of Reproductive Genetic Technologies Express Disvalue for People with Disabilities?" *Journal of Medical Ethics* 36 (2010): 217–21.

Elizabeth Marquardt, Norval D. Glenn, and Karen Clark. *My Daddy's Name Is Donor: A New Study of Young Adults Conceived through Sperm Donation*. New York: Institute for American Values, 2010.

Gilbert Meilaender. *Bioethics: A Primer for Christians*. Grand Rapids: Wm. B. Eerdmans Publishing Co., 1996.

Bonnie J. Miller-McLemore. "'Let the Children Come' Revisited." In *The Child in Christian Thought*, edited by Marcia J. Bunge, 446–73. Grand Rapids: Wm. B. Eerdmans Publishing Co., 2001.

Liza Mundy. *Everything Conceivable: How Assisted Reproduction Is Changing the World*. New York: Alfred A. Knopf, 2007.

Oliver O'Donovan. "In a Glass Darkly." In *On Moral Medicine*, edited by Stephen E. Lammers and Allen Verhey, 496–505. Grand Rapids: Wm. B. Eerdmans Publishing Co., 1998.

Peggy Orenstein. *Waiting for Daisy: A Tale of Two Continents, Three Religions, Five Infertility Doctors, an Oscar, an Atomic Bomb, a Romantic Night, and One Woman's Quest to Become a Mother*. New York: Bloomsbury, 2007.

Kate M. Ott. *A Time to Be Born: A Faith-Based Guide to Assisted Reproductive Technology*. Westport, CT: The Religious Institute, 2009.

Anna Poulson. "Maybe Baby." *Third Way* 26, no. 2 (2003): 12–14.

Hans Reinders. "Life's Goodness: On Disability, Genetics, and 'Choice.'" In *Theology, Disability, and the New Genetics: Why Science Needs the Church*, edited by John Swinton and Brian Brock, 163–81. New York: Continuum, 2007.

Bonnie J. Rough. *Carrier: Untangling the Danger in My DNA*. Berkeley, CA: Counterpoint, 2010.

Maura A. Ryan. *Ethics and Economics of Assisted Reproduction: The Cost of Longing*. Washington, DC: Georgetown University Press, 2001.

Laurie Strongin. *Saving Henry: A Mother's Journey*. New York: Hyperion, 2010.

John Swinton. "Introduction: Re-imagining Genetics and Disability." In *Theology, Disability, and the New Genetics: Why Science Needs the Church*, edited by John Swinton and Brian Brock, 1–25. New York: Continuum, 2007.

John Swinton and Brian Brock, eds. *Theology, Disability, and the New Genetics: Why Science Needs the Church*. New York: Continuum, 2007.

U.S. Conference of Catholic Bishops. *Life-Giving Love in an Age of Technology*. November 17, 2009. http://www.usccb.org/LifeGivingLove/lifegivinglovedocument.pdf.

Yuri Verlinsky and Anver Kuliev. "Ethical, Social, and Legal Issues." In *Practical Preimplantation Genetic Diagnosis*. London: Springer-Verlag, 2005.

Ayelet Waldman. *Bad Mother: A Chronicle of Maternal Crimes, Minor Calamities, and Occasional Moments of Grace*. New York: Doubleday, 2009.

Alice Wexler. *Mapping Fate: A Memoir of Family, Risk, and Genetic Research*. Berkeley: University of California Press, 1995.

Mitchell Zuckoff. *Choosing Naia: A Family's Journey*. Boston: Beacon Press, 2002.

Index

CPSIA information can be obtained at www.ICGtesting.com
Printed in the USA
LVOW080433240112

265211LV00004B/1/P